Becoming
the Person God
Wants You to Be

Becoming the Person God Wants You to Be

Understanding the Journey from Shadow to Substance

Gabriel Alonso

New Wine Press

New Wine Ministries
PO Box 17
Chichester
West Sussex
United Kingdom
PO20 6YB

ISBN 1–903725–52–6

Typeset by CRB Associates, Reepham, Norfolk
Cover design by CCD, www.ccdgroup.co.uk
Printed in Malta

Contents

	Commendations	7
Chapter 1	Shadow and Substance	9
Chapter 2	Biblical Examples of Types and Shadows from the Old Testament Revealed in the New Testament	21
Chapter 3	How Do We Apply This in Our Own Lives?	29
Chapter 4	Signposts to the Substance	33
Chapter 5	Moving from Shadow to Substance	43
Chapter 6	Why is it So Important to Move into the Substance?	57
Chapter 7	Things to Consider When Moving from the Shadow to the Substance	69
Chapter 8	Obstacles That Can Prevent Us Moving from Shadow to Substance	83
Chapter 9	The Temptation to Want to Be Someone Else	109
	Conclusion	119
	Acknowledgments	123
	About the Author	126

Commendations for *Becoming the Person God Wants You to Be*

"Looking for one's purpose or destiny can be exciting, puzzling and frustrating all at the same time! Failure to find one is ultimately tragic, but can we be sure that one even exists? Whether you are just setting out to discover it or doing a course-check mid-journey, this book is full of hope, encouragement and keys to understand and unlock the potential of your life."

Graham Kendrick
Songwriter, worship leader

"So many people live in shadows, never coming to the full realisation of who they are and what they can do. Gabriel Alonso, in both his life and teaching has addressed these issues. He is an honourable and clear thinking man who, alongside his career as a professional musician, has revelation in teaching the Scriptures."

David Shearman
Senior Minister, Christian Centre, Nottingham

Chapter 1

Shadow and Substance

It was an evening rehearsal and I sat, as usual, behind my timpani. We were all waiting for the conductor to arrive so we could start rehearsing for our next concert. My mind wandered back over the years. I was trying to find in my "yesterdays" some answers for my "tomorrow" and I found myself drifting back to the town of Annecy in south east France, where I was born. Annecy is a beautiful place surrounded by mountains and blessed with picturesque valleys and lakes. It was the place where, at an early age, I became passionately interested in music. My dad was a drummer and I remember as a little boy spending much of my time in rehearsal rooms while he was practising. At the age of ten I began learning to play the drums myself and I went to the local conservatoire to study orchestral percussion and music theory. Eventually, with the help of many gifted people who tutored me through extensive training, this led me into a career as a professional musician. I began work as a percussion teacher at the Conservatoire National de Region de Grenoble. I was also head of Percussion at the Jazz department of nearby Chambery, and timpanist with the Grenoble Symphonic Orchestra.

Still daydreaming, I recalled a trip to Caracas in Venezuela where, at a time when I was really questioning what life was all about, I gave my life to the Lord. Before coming to Christ I had felt empty and dissatisfied with my career. Not only that, but I had met numbers of artists who were equally dissatisfied and searching for meaning.

I was quickly brought back to the present by the oboe playing a sustained A note. The whole orchestra began tuning to it, demonstrating that music really is "The art of combining sounds and rhythm in a manner that is enjoyable to the ear." Using the oboe as my reference note, I carefully began to tune my instruments.[1] Little did I know that something was about to happen that would change my whole life . . . and my understanding about destiny! At that very moment a thought struck me: "What you are doing now is the shadow of things to come . . ."

This thought made a very strong impression on me and I was unable to think about anything else for a few days. It was not the result of my personal meditations or any conversation I'd had with anybody, but this thought, that I did not fully understand, was ever present, constantly resounding in my spirit like a cymbal.

It was my burning bush! I was intrigued by this thought that refused to go away and would not burn up and disappear in smoke like some of my other ideas. The Lord had clearly got my attention and in the coming days, as I began to pray about it and approach this "idea", He spoke to me and gave me the revelation and understanding I was looking for. (Remember that it was only as Moses *approached* the burning bush that God spoke to him. Too many people contemplate what is burning in them, but they don't move; they dare not take a step towards it. But the bush will just keep on burning; the thought, the vision in you will not be consumed! If that is you, then approach it my friend!)

I realised that I was standing on "holy ground" as it were, about to enter a new phase in my life. Consequently, it came as no surprise when, in 1993, the Lord asked me to leave my country, my "father's house", my job, my career, my friends – absolutely everything! – and move to England. And so it was that I found myself going to serve a man of God who is the senior pastor of a large church in Nottingham. Many people around me could not understand why I was leaving France, and although I could feel the Spirit leading me, it seemed crazy to me too! There seemed to be no sense in it. I had spent years building my reputation as a musician, my career as a percussion teacher in the Conservatoire, the Orchestra, the Jazz department. Many said, "You can continue serving God in your career as a musician." In one sense of course, what they said was true, but deep in my heart I knew I needed to believe, obey God's word to me, and see with the eyes of faith. I went over and over the words: "This is the shadow of things to come." I wanted to leave the shadow and live in the substance of what the Lord had prepared for me.

On the 4th of June of 1994, in the living room of our rented house in England, my wife Andrea and I were watching the commemoration of the fiftieth anniversary of D-Day on television and I found myself weeping uncontrollably. I thought about all those young men fighting on the French beaches to deliver my nation. I heard accounts of General Charles De Gaulle calling to the French on the radio to come and join him and become "the free forces". Once again those words of the Lord came to me: "This is the shadow of the things to come."

As a result of this encounter with the Lord, my wife and I were moved to establish a leadership training school in England called "EDMF" (Ecole des Ministeres Francophones) which means "School of Ministries for French speaking Leaders". We feel that God has called us to minister especially among French speaking nations and to help people to discover their destiny in Christ. People from these nations come to seek the Lord with us and to find out what their calling is. I can look back and say that I am so glad I obeyed His voice. It was scary, it seemed crazy, but His voice was stronger than all my fears. Don't ever let the fear of failure stop you from obeying.

Andrea and I now travel the world teaching Christians and non-Christians how to live the life they were born to live. Many people know so little about themselves that they fail to make the connection between what they are and what they could be – between the *shadow* and the *substance*. They don't understand this principle and have never even been taught it.

In this book we will explore that connection between shadow and substance and give practical examples that will help you to move from where you are now into your God-given calling and destiny, through Christ – the door that gives us access to the substance of our lives.

The Bible allows us to catch a glimpse of these two worlds and gives numerous examples of shadows and substance, and of individuals who moved from one into the other to become great men and women of God, setting an example for us all.

Somebody once told me not to preach or teach certain principles unless I have experienced them myself. In other words, if you haven't actually done yourself what you are talking about, you are only *assuming* that you understand the full implications of your message, and therefore have far less authority. I try to live by this principle, so what I am about to open up in this book is not only my own experience and journey with the Lord, but also that of many other believers I know personally who have gone through the same process. As we read on and pull out into deeper waters, I pray that the eyes of our hearts will be enlightened so that we may know the hope to which He has called us all. May these few lines help many more to catch a glimpse of the substance awaiting them in Christ. My desire is to help you to get there more quickly than I did!

Shadow and substance

I would like to lay a strong foundation to support everything we are about to consider. Before we can understand the "things to come", we need to look at the concept of "shadows".

What is a shadow?

It is not darkness! Darkness and shadows are two different things. Being in the dark and being in the shade is different isn't it? Darkness is the absence of light, but a shadow implies that there is a source of light somewhere. In the spiritual world, darkness also represents the absence of light (which is Christ) and the Bible symbolises darkness as living without the knowledge of God; consciously or unconsciously living without obeying Him. Darkness is a place where God is absent (symbolically, because God can *never* be absent!)

> "... *him who called you out of darkness into his wonderful light.*"
>
> (1 Peter 2:9)

Now let's go back to the natural. Shade or a shadow occurs when light is obstructed. For example, if I put my hand in front of a light, a shadow is produced on the wall. The shadow is the same shape as the object, but it has no substance. The shadow of my hand on the wall is the same shape as my hand, but it is only

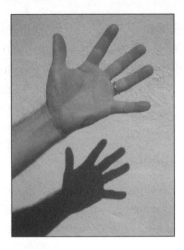

Figure 1: Substance, light and shadow

a "hand without substance". The object causing the shadow *is* the substance (my hand is the object, the substance causing the shadow). The closer the object moves to the light, the more blurred the shape of the shadow becomes. If you hold a pen in front of a light, the pen's shadow appears on the wall. If you move the pen closer to the light and further away from the wall, the shadow gradually loses its clarity.

To summarise then (see figure 1),

- A shadow has no substance, it is not the real thing, just a shape, a copy, a silhouette of the real thing.
- Substance is found between the light and the shadow.

This natural law of physics is also a spiritual law.

Two worlds

The Greeks had a fundamental belief concerning the universe. They believed in two worlds, one real and one unreal. They believed that the world of space and time was nothing more than a pale copy of the real world.

This was Plato's philosophy, the greatest Greek thinker. He believed in what he called "The Shapes" – that somewhere there was a world where perfect shapes existed, of which the human world was an imperfect copy. He believed for example, that somewhere there existed the perfect shape of a chair and that all the chairs of this world were nothing more than imperfect copies of it; he believed that there was a "perfect" horse and that all other horses were poor copies, and so on.

The Greeks were fascinated by this theory of a "real" world and its poor reflection and they thought that death was merely a bridge between one world and the other. That was their belief! But we who are in Christ, are not talking about mystical ideas from ancient Greece, nor are we talking about an inaccessible world. Rather, we are talking about entering into the *real substance* of what Christ has prepared for us here *on this earth*. We are talking about a real world; a world of obedience to the Master, a world of destiny, fulfilment, joy, and yes, a world of trials too; a world that is accessible to anyone who is a new creation in Christ.

The principle of shadow and substance is a biblical one, not a manmade principle. It is found in the Word of God as we will see now.

The word for shadow in Hebrew is *skia* (pronounced skee'-ah). It is defined as,

- Shade caused by the interception of light
- An image cast by an object and representing the form of that object
- A sketch, outline, adumbration

The Old Testament law as a shadow

> *"These* [laws and regulations] *are a **shadow** of the things that were to come; the reality* [the body, the substance]*, however, is found in Christ."*
>
> (Colossians 2:17, emphasis added)

> *"The law is only a **shadow** of the good things that are coming –* not the realities [substance] *themselves."*
>
> (Hebrews 10:1)

The priesthood and sanctuaries are shadows

Even the Old Testament high priest who was appointed to offer both gifts and sacrifices to the Lord was a shadow of the things to come. He was a type of Christ, a shadow of the One who is our High Priest, who sat down at the right hand of the throne of the Majesty in heaven (Hebrews 8:1). The tabernacle, or the sanctuary was also a shadow of the things to come, as the Bible tells us in Hebrews 8:5:

> *"They* [the priests] *serve at a sanctuary that is a copy and **shadow** of what is in heaven. This is why Moses was warned when he was about to build the tabernacle: 'See to it that you make everything according to the pattern shown you on the mountain.'"*
>
> (emphasis added)

Whether Moses had a revelation of the heavenly tabernacle or diligently followed a blueprint shown to him on the mountain we do not know, but the fact is he built a tabernacle that was a shadow, a copy of what is in heaven. But if the substance is in heaven, what exactly is it? What kind of sanctuary or temple is found in heaven? The Bible gives us an amazing insight in Revelation 21:2–3. The apostle John, transported into an awesome vision, says,

> *"I saw the Holy City, the new Jerusalem, coming down out of heaven from God, prepared as a bride beautifully dressed for her husband. And I heard a loud voice from the throne saying, 'Now the dwelling* [tabernacle] *of God is with men, and he will live with them. They will be his people, and God himself will be with them and be their God.' "*

The sanctuary, the tabernacle in heaven is nothing less than the new Jerusalem, the dwelling place of God and this is what Scripture says about our future dwelling place:

> *"The city does not need the sun or the moon to shine on it, for the glory of God gives it light, and the Lamb is its lamp."*
>
> (Revelation 21:23)

Now we understand where the shadow (the sanctuary on earth) comes from. Remember that a shadow is caused by an object obstructing light. The Lamb of God is the lamp of the city (the word indicates a candle that is placed on a stand or candlestick) and the glory of God gives light to the city. Both the "lamp" and the "glory" are shining on the city creating a shadow and projecting it. Where? On earth! The shadow has the same "shape" or silhouette as the object causing it. In heaven the glory of God and the brilliant splendour of the Lamb are shining on the holy tabernacle of God, and from heaven its shadow is cast onto the earth, a silhouette of the glorious temple that we will see one day.

Many are those who have seen things in shadow, but some have looked through the eyes of faith and have seen beyond the shadow to the substance. The Bible says that by faith Abraham made his home in the Promised Land like a stranger in a foreign country. He lived in tents, as did Isaac and Jacob, who were heirs with him of the same promise. He was looking towards the city (the new Jerusalem) with foundations, whose architect and builder is God (Hebrews 11:9). What about Moses? He too was looking ahead to his reward. By faith he left Egypt, not fearing the king's anger and he persevered because he saw the One who is invisible (Hebrews 11:26–27). Moses, King David and Herod worked hard to build a sanctuary, but it was only a shadow of the substance that is found in heaven.

It is fascinating to note that all the sanctuaries (the tabernacle, the first temple, and the second temple) were built with their main entrance facing east. Another word used for "east" is "orient", so we can say that each sanctuary was well orientated, facing the rising sun in the morning and the promise of a new day and of better things to come. Their natural position and orientation were a symbolic shadow of things to come, a copy of what is in heaven.

The worship and songs performed in the earthly temples were also a pale reflection of what is happening in heaven. It is my conviction that today our worship, adoration and music can be a shadow of what is happening in heaven. Through the Spirit of God we need to tune our ears to hear the sound of heaven so that we will be God's orchestra. It seems to me that the more the prophets and the musicians come together, working, praying, interceding and travailing together, the more likely we are to hear a different sound of worship on earth. One which could move us from shadow to substance. We will come back to this later.

In chapter 3 we will go on to apply the principles of shadow and substance to our own lives, but before we do, in the next chapter I want us to look at some examples from the Bible of people or situations that were shadows of the things to come.

Note
1. To tune timpani, apart from needing a good musical ear to pitch the note, you need to lean over the instrument and place your ear a couple of centimetres from the head of the timp, flicking it gently with your finger so that you can hear the note without disturbing the other musicians in the orchestra. You tune the timp by pressing or releasing a pedal situated at the bottom of the drum. Pressing the pedal increases the tension of the head and the sound sharpens; releasing the pedal decreases the tension of the head and the sound flattens. If you do this for each of your timpani (two to six per timpanist), you can play in any key and you can quickly and quietly tune up while the rest of the orchestra is playing.

Chapter 2

Biblical Examples of Types and Shadows from the Old Testament Revealed in the New Testament

Abraham sacrifices his son Isaac (Genesis 22)

Abraham was told by the Lord to offer his son Isaac as a burnt offering to Him. The Bible tells us in verse 3 of Genesis chapter 22 that early the next morning Abraham got up, saddled his donkey, and took two servants and his son Isaac with him. When he had cut enough wood for the burnt offering he set out for the place God had told him. Abraham gave Isaac the wood to carry. The wood that Isaac carried on his back was a shadow of things to come. It was a picture of Jesus Christ carrying the cross (the wood) to the place where He was to be crucified. It was a shadow of the Father sacrificing His only son for the sin of the world. Isaac carrying the wood was the shadow, Christ carrying the cross was the substance.

In verse 7 Isaac begins to question his father. "Father?" he inquired. "Yes, my son?" Abraham replied. "The fire and wood are here," Isaac said, "but where is the lamb for the burnt offering?" Abraham answered, "God himself will provide the lamb for the burnt offering, my son."

This again is a shadow of the things to come. There was no lamb to be found. The animal that Abraham actually sacrificed was a ram, not a lamb. Abraham said that God Himself would provide the lamb, and He did. A few centuries later John the Baptist stood in the river Jordan, baptising those who believed in the coming of the kingdom of God and he saw a man coming towards him. As his heart began to beat faster and faster, he recognised Him and said to his disciples: *"Look, the Lamb of God, who takes away the sin of the world!"* Here was the lamb for the offering. Here was the lamb Isaac mentioned, the sacrifice that Abraham was talking about hundreds of years before. Here was the substance. Abraham's ram was but a shadow. How I would have loved to see John the Baptist's face when He saw Jesus, the substance that all the prophets before him had longed to see!

The ram that Abraham saw caught in a thicket by its horns is also a shadow of the Saviour – the lamb of God wearing a crown of thorns that the Roman soldiers twisted together and put on His head (John 19:2).

Moses: a type of Jesus

Moses was a type of Jesus. He was a foreshadow of the coming Saviour whose mission was to bring his people out of slavery in Egypt and into the Promised Land. Jesus brought us out of the slavery of sin. He broke the power that Satan, the pharaoh of this world, had over us.

In Exodus 32:32 Moses intercedes on behalf of the people, a foreshadow of the ministry of Jesus today, who intercedes to the Father on our behalf.

The journey to the Promised Land is also a shadow of what we are called to do. Moses led the people through the Red Sea and we also must go through the "Red Sea", symbolised by the act of being baptised in water.

The Lord gave the Israelites the Torah at Sinai. In the same way we receive His Word, the Bible, when we accept Jesus as our Lord. The Israelites had the Promised Land in sight, it was the place the Lord had prepared for them, but they never entered it because their faith crumbled when they saw the giants. Equally, we have a "Promised Land" that was prepared for us before the foundation of the earth. It is not a physical place, but rather the works that God has prepared for us to do. It is what we were meant to be in Christ. This is our Promised Land and not enough Christians understand this; not enough leaders teach this foundation of the Christian life. The result is that far too many Christians stay wandering about in the desert and sometimes die there, missing out on all the wonderful promises God has for them, falling short of the substance of their lives. Of course, we can be saved in the desert and God provides for all our needs there, for sure. The Israelites had clothing and food which was given day after day, but the manna was temporary food and could not be compared to the food waiting for them in the Promised Land!

How many Christians feel ready to do God's will, but change their minds when they see the giants standing on the border of their Promised Land? Giants of fear that tell them "God will never provide for you if you step out in faith." Giants of "insecurity", giants of "lack of confidence", giants of "what other people will think of you" etc. The list could go on, but the purpose here is to show that the things that happened to the Israelites were a shadow of what we have to go through today and are warnings for us all. The apostle Paul puts it this way:

"For I do not want you to be ignorant of the fact, brothers, that our forefathers were all under the cloud and that they all passed through the sea. They were all baptised into Moses in the cloud and in the sea. They all ate the same spiritual food and drank the same spiritual drink; for they drank from the spiritual rock that accompanied them, and that rock was Christ. Nevertheless, God was not pleased with most of them; their bodies were scattered over the desert. Now these things occurred as examples [type, print, shadows] *to keep us from setting our hearts on evil things as they did."*

(1 Corinthians 10:1–6)

There, above the cover

One of my favourite examples of a shadow was when the Lord spoke to Moses in Exodus 25:22 and said:

"There, above the cover between the two cherubim that are over the ark of the Testimony, I will meet with you and give you all my commands for the Israelites."

Here is the shadow of something that happened to **Mary Magdalene** when she went to the tomb where Jesus was buried. She saw that the stone had been rolled away from the entrance and after she had told Peter and John, the three of them went back to the tomb. Soon Peter and John went home and Mary was left weeping by the empty tomb. John chapter 20 tells us:

"As she wept, she bent over to look into the tomb and saw two angels [the two cherubim] *in white, seated where Jesus' body had been, one at the head and the other at the foot* ['between the two cherubim'].

They asked her, 'Woman, why are you crying?'

"They have taken my Lord away,' she replied, 'and I don't know where they have put him.' At this, she turned round and saw Jesus standing there, but she did not realise that it was Jesus.

'Woman,' he said, 'why are you crying? Who is it you are looking for?'

Thinking he was the gardener, she said, 'Sir, if you have carried him away, tell me where you have put him, and I will get him."

Jesus said to her, 'Mary.'

She turned towards him and cried out in Aramaic, 'Rabboni!' (which means Teacher).

Jesus said, 'Do not hold on to me, for I have not yet returned to the Father. Go instead to my brothers and tell them, "I am returning to my Father and your Father, to my God and your God."' "

(John 20:11–17)

There, between the two cherubim as it were, she was told what to do. Moses received a promise in the same way, that from between the two cherubim God would meet with him and give him his commands.

We could also mention **David**. When he was discussing a way to get rid of Goliath with King Saul, he described the years of looking after his father's sheep as years of preparation for the great day. Here is what he actually said to Saul:

"Your servant has been keeping his father's sheep. When a lion or a bear came and carried off a sheep from the flock, I went after it, struck it and rescued the sheep from its mouth. When it turned on me, I seized it by its hair, struck it and killed it. Your servant has killed both the lion and the bear; this uncircumcised

Philistine will be like one of them, because he has defied the
armies of the living God."

(1 Samuel 17:34–36)

The things that happened to David as a boy were the shadow of
things to come for him. He was shepherd of his father's sheep as
a boy, and he became the shepherd of the people of God. He was
also a shadow of Jesus the Good Shepherd.

What about **Amos**, a shepherd who also took care of
sycamore-fig trees? When he was challenged by Amaziah the
priest, he argued that he was neither a prophet nor a son of a
prophet. Nevertheless the Lord took him away from his sheep
and said to him, *"Go, prophesy to my people Israel"* (Amos 7:15).
The interesting thing about a sycamore-fig tree is that it
produces fruit that is sometimes referred to as "Egyptian figs".
These particular figs have to be carefully cultivated by making
incisions in them; they are cut or scored with a knife and four
days after being scored, they ripen!

The relationship between Amos' job and what God called him
to do (shadow and substance) is very interesting. I wonder if he
ever thought about the similarity between the two? Sometimes
strong words that cut to the heart are needed, so that the people
will fulfil all the potential that is in them (i.e. causing them
to "ripen"). We are often too nice to people! It may seem like
the best way at the time, but it could mean the death of all the
potential in them. Amos was called to cut, to make an incision,
so that the people would return to God. Amos was called to be
a plumb-line among Israel. As a good friend of mine puts it, he
was called to show that the wall of their lives was not straight!
That's the purpose of a plumb-line isn't it? It tells you if you are
building "true" or not. It is very clear and there is no way
around it.

Amos also functioned as a shepherd. If only all prophets had a bit more concern for the flock of God! How many people have we seen cut open by the word of a prophet and then left to bleed to death?

Amos' "secular" job foreshadowed his ministry as a prophet and the manner in which he would fulfil it: Cutting and caring! Strong, but comforting.

All examples of types and shadows were revealed through people by who they were and what they did. In the next chapter we will look at how to apply this principle to our own lives.

Chapter 3

How Do We Apply This in Our Own Lives?

So what about us? How do we apply all this to our own lives? What is the "shadow" and what is the "substance" in your life?

We have seen through various examples from the Bible that the shadow has the same "shape" (silhouette) as the object causing it, but a shadow has no substance. We also know that we get nowhere by remaining in the shadows; our calling is not to stay in the wilderness! The purpose of a life in God is to get into the substance.

Here is our first challenge: a Christian can be operating in the "shadow", perhaps without realising it. In other words, although his identity and activities look like substance, they are in fact shadow. Substance is our spiritual identity – the works we are called and equipped to accomplish. How do you make sure that you are not operating in the shadow? By moving closer to the light. The shadow of an object loses clarity the nearer you move to the light. So, the more you approach Christ (the light), the more you move into the substance of what you are in Him and into the things He has prepared for you. The shadow, or what you were doing before, quickly loses its appeal!

When I was tuning my timpani that evening at the rehearsal and the Lord spoke to me about the shadow of the things to come, I began to see the orchestra as a shadow of the Church: all its "living stone" members in the right place, using their gifts; their instruments in tune with the oboe, the Spirit of God, and all working under the direction of the conductor, Christ, head of His divine orchestra and ambassador of the most beautiful melody on earth.

I have imagined this scenario many times:

It is just moments before a concert is due to begin. The concert hall is packed with people, still chatting and excited at the prospect of the concert. Then the oboe plays an A note and everybody stops to listen, including the crowd. Everyone tunes up, starting with the woodwind, then the brass, then the timps, and finally the strings. The choir stands expectantly behind the musicians. When everybody is ready, a heavy silence falls in the hall. Everyone is waiting for the one who will lead the orchestra, the one who will decide on the tempo, nuances and intensity of the music, the one who will be the heart and soul of the orchestra, the conductor.

He steps onto the stage, the audience applaud and the orchestra stands respectfully. He greets the audience then turns to the orchestra. With a wave of his hand he invites them to be seated. Everyone holds their breath as they wait for the first movement of his baton. Time stands still ... nothing moves on stage or in the audience. There is still a few seconds for the orchestra to meditate on the practice they have put in for what they are about to play, but it is far too late to change anything now. Then, with a smile, the conductor ignites the orchestra and the choir and the sound fills the concert hall; the tension of the build up is released.

The Bible tells us that Jesus is coming back for us. The Great Conductor is coming back for His orchestra. He is expecting us to be in tune with His oboe, the Holy Spirit. He is also expecting us to play the correct instrument and the correct music skilfully. When He steps on stage, He will lead us into the most awesome concerto, the concerto for Judgment Day! This final piece will not be in G minor but in Jesus Major! The Jesus who is coming back will not be a little baby, or be riding peacefully on a donkey, but riding a white horse, the Lord of hosts, the One who will bring all things in heaven and on earth together under one head, even Christ. The earth will be filled with the song of the Lord and we will all sing His glory along with the angelic choir. The One who said to me: "What you are doing now is the shadow of the things to come" is calling us to leave the shadow and find the substance of our life. He is calling us to learn how to tune to Him, how to hear the Spirit, how to hear the oboe of God. He wants us to know our role in the great orchestra, to submit to the first violin (next in line to the conductor), to respect the nuances in the Word of God, the timing and the different colours of sound, to know the way the Great Conductor moves, talks and looks at us; to fix our eyes on His hands and follow His baton. We must learn how to recognise and develop gifts in others, so that they can move into the substance of their lives too and be effective in the kingdom of God. You may be a nurse or a doctor, maybe you are a manager, a salesman or a school teacher, an electrician or a musician ... let's look beyond this.

I know several school teachers who are great Bible teachers. I have seen nurses with extraordinary pastoral gifting which comes from a genuine desire to care for the people of God. Look for the common denominator between what you do in the natural and what you could be doing in the spiritual. Look for the common denominator between shadow and substance, bearing in mind that the shadow has the same shape as the substance.

In the next chapter we will continue looking at how to apply this principle in our own lives by looking at a number of "signposts" that will lead us towards the substance of our lives.

Chapter 4

Signposts to the Substance

Gifts

Our God-given gifts are a strong indication of our destiny in Christ. Our destiny is the substance of what we are called to. We could also call it our potential. Our gifts have the "flavour" of what God has called us to do, they form part of the shadow of things to come.

Our gifts are given to us by our Father in heaven so that we can fulfil our potential, reaching the substance of our calling and identity in Christ. Our responsibility is to develop these gifts so that we can fulfil our mission on earth, prepared for us before the creation of the world (Ephesians 2:10).

We can summarise it like this: Before the creation of the world, God saw you and He prepared works for you to do. He did all this *in love* (Ephesians 1:4).

God has given you all the necessary tools (gifts) so that your works can be done with excellence and bring Him glory. There is a direct link between the gifts you possess and the works God has prepared for you. Gifts are a good indication of what you are supposed to be doing, since they were given to you for that very purpose!

It is my conviction that our gifts are given to us even before we meet Christ, because the work prepared for us (the substance) was already in God's mind before the creation of the world. It is not a biblical view to believe that it is only at the point when you come to Christ and accept Him as your Lord and Saviour that He gives you the gifts you need to serve Him. It is true that the Lord gives you spiritual gifts when you acknowledge Him as the Lord of your life, but I am not talking about gifts of the Spirit here, but natural gifts. When Jesus becomes your Lord and Saviour He gives you additional gifts of the Spirit which enhance the natural gifts He prepared for you before you were born! When you use your natural gifts, God's Spirit working through you can totally change the atmosphere in a place.

How many lives have been hindered by a misunderstanding of this foundational truth? How many gifted people have heard their pastor saying that they should give up music or painting or their career in sport, or dance, because these things "belong to the past"?! How many frustrated artists do we have in our congregations? These natural gifts are given to us so that we can live in the substance of what God has ordained for us. They were "given" before we ever met Jesus and go hand in hand with the works God prepared for us to do. Here is what the Lord said to Jeremiah:

> *"Before I formed you in the womb I knew you,*
>   *before you were born I set you apart;*
>   *I appointed you as a prophet to the nations."*

(Jeremiah 1:5)

The Lord knew Jeremiah before he was even born – his mission, his potential, his substance was prepared before he was born, with all the gifts he would need. We will see later that gifts need to be discovered and developed, but for now let us simply remember that they go hand in hand with the mission assigned for us.

Let me tell you a story that will illustrate this very well:

When I was in primary school, there was a boy in my class called Jean Pierre who was a very gifted communicator. The teacher was impressed with our class-mate who was in his element whenever he was given the chance to speak to the class. Jean Pierre shone each time he was called out to the front to explain something. He would deliver his given theme in such a way that his story literally came to life. We entered his world and held our breath in suspense if he so wished. He was so convincing. This also made him the best liar in the whole school!

When we left primary school to go to high school I lost track of him. However, I never forgot Jean Pierre, he made such an impression upon me as a brilliant communicator at such a young age. Many years later I saw him again and was not in the least surprised to see the profession he had chosen. The very same Jean Pierre who was so convincing, holding everyone's attention, had become a car salesman! Jean Pierre had an extraordinary gift of communication. This grace (and it is grace, since the gift depends on the giver not the receiver) was given to him by God so that Jean Pierre might fulfil his potential in life – the things prepared in advance for him to do before the foundation of the world. Even though Jean Pierre is not in Christ he still uses his natural God-given gift, but in the wrong domain, because he still does not know God. He uses his gift of communication to convince people to buy his cars! He must be good because even my dad, who is a tough nut to crack, was totally convinced and bought one!

Of course, I am not saying that selling cars is not a "worthy" activity in God's eyes. As part of the plan of God it could be a wonderful ministry and a powerful and effective means of serving Him by sharing our testimony with others. But I see a Jean Pierre who could be saved and called to the things God has prepared for him. God has given him the necessary gifts to accomplish that task.

My conviction is that like many others (Christians and non-Christians alike), Jean Pierre is using his gift in the wrong domain. He is living in the shadow and not in the substance. The plans God has for Jean Pierre are still waiting for him. The Bible says that, *"The plans of the* LORD *stand firm for ever ..."* (Psalm 33:11). With the eyes of the Spirit I can see him saved, in Christ, in his substance, a preacher, an evangelist or a prophet, or an MP perhaps? A son of the kingdom, busy doing kingdom jobs that God has placed in his life. I see him walking in the things he was born to do, using his God-given gift of communication and fulfilling his potential. Let us hope that many like him will come to know Jesus and fulfil their destiny using the gifts God has blessed them with.

A child's natural gifts begin to emerge at a very early age. Because of the many activities a child is involved in at school, teachers begin to see the tip of the iceberg of their gifts emerging. During their school years a child is placed in many situations and environments: studying, reading, performing in front of others, sports, competition, music etc. Walking this long path of apprenticeship, the child is trained, sharpened, challenged and hopefully inspired by some of the things he is asked to do. School and later, university, should provide a strong foundation in education, but should also confirm in a child's mind and heart the things he aspires to and feels gifted for.

I was talking with some friends recently whose son really

enjoys playing the drums, but they think he should also try percussion. They were asking me what was the best thing to do, not wanting to confuse him by offering too much choice. My suggestion was to place him in a variety of situations where he could hear good drummers and alternatively hear orchestral percussion and see what his reaction would be.

What is true for a child remains true for an adult. Even though it is better to start at an early age, it is possible to discover your gifts and develop them later in life. When I was studying music in the Conservatoire National Superieur De Musique De Paris I had a friend who was following the same programme as I was, aiming for the same degree. He started studying percussion at the age of twenty-two, whereas I had started when I was ten! Some of the greatest jazz musicians started to study at a very late stage in their lives.

Deep calls to deep

Another signpost to our substance is the way we react when we come into contact with the very thing that we will, or ought to be doing. I remember one particular day when my dad was on stage playing drums with his band. When I heard him playing my "substance" stirred within me. It was like an echo in my young heart.

I remember my dad travelling around France and abroad as a drummer and it had a powerful impact on me. A taste for adventure began to grow and I wanted to travel more and more. I remember riding my moped along unknown roads, discovering new villages out in the country. Years later I felt the same impact when I listened to a man preaching from the Bible. I could see myself in his shoes and I felt a tremendous joy. Today I travel a lot playing music and teaching the Bible and I often think back to those first "echoes" I felt in my heart as a little boy as I came into contact with the things that were in store for my future!

I am a great believer that the best "mentors" are those who are called to the same mission as those they train. The Elijah-Elisha model is the best one in my opinion, though not everybody is fortunate enough to find such a good role model. Later, we will look at this more closely as we talk about sharpening our gifts. For now, we need to realise that our potential, the substance prepared for us, lies deep inside us like a seed in the ground. Once this potential is exposed to something of its own kind, it begins to move and grow, like a seed that only needs to be watered by a gardener.

Another example of this principle is when somebody's potential comes into contact with the very reason it was given in the first place. It begins to cry out, saying: "Here I am! Here I am!" The Bible calls this "deep calling to deep":

> *"Deep calls to deep*
>   *in the roar of your waterfalls."*
>
> (Psalm 42:7)

"The roar of your waterfalls" is God's voice calling to the deep (the substance) that He has planted in the soil of your life.

When Samson was in Mahaneh Dan (Judges 13:25), the Bible says that the Spirit of the Lord began to stir him. Why there? Because in Mahaneh Dan, the Philistines had built a stronghold. Samson's life calling was to defeat the Philistines and there he was, faced with the very reason he was born and he felt the stirring of the Spirit of God. The circumstances he found himself in were calling to the "deep" – his purpose in life.

When Moses, who's calling was to deliver his people from slavery, saw an Egyptian beating a Hebrew (Exodus 2:11), he was exposed to the very reason he was born. Something stirred in him and he could not help but act. Forty years of growing up in Egypt had not killed the seed in Moses. He was exposed to his potential at the age of forty. That's when the substance of what he was called to be cried out in him louder than anything else; louder than his position as prince of Egypt; louder than his Egyptian education. His call to be the deliverer of the Hebrews shook his world and emerged from his innermost being. That was his mission in life, his substance! Moses was responding to what he saw: an Egyptian beating a Hebrew. He responded in a very radical way; he didn't think, but was overwhelmed, I believe, by the substance of his calling in God. He could not help but start the process by freeing at least *one* of his Hebrew brothers.

John the Baptist's calling was to announce the coming of the Messiah. As his mother Elizabeth carried him in her womb, she met with Mary who was carrying the unborn Jesus. John the Baptist leapt in his mother's womb at that meeting! He had come into contact with his destiny.

This process of deep calling to deep is not bound by age. The Lord's plans for your life will always prevail. The only danger is that potential will remain just potential if it is not developed, but age should not stop us. A young person has more time and energy to develop his gifts and achieve his potential, but you are in no way disqualified as you get older. Look at Moses. He was eighty years old when he was told what his mission in life would be!

Jesus saw the substance of His life at a very early age. When He was twelve He told His parents, who had lost Him in Jerusalem, *"Why did you seek Me? Did you not know that I must be about My Father's business?"* (Luke 2:49 NKJV)

The young Jesus had an understanding of the things He was

called to do (His Father's business). When He was in the temple discussing issues with the teachers of the law, He was confronted with Himself! The Lamb of God! At this stage of His life Scripture would have been like a mirror before His face.

Once we understand this principle and the wonderful deposit of purpose and gifts the Lord has put in every human being, then we do not see unsaved people in the same way as we used to. We begin to see them as "potential" waiting to be stirred for the kingdom. In this way Jesus saw Peter's potential and never stopped believing in him because He had seen the substance He was calling Peter into.

The desires of your heart

My wife Andrea and I live in West Yorkshire, England, and a few years ago several hectares of land close to where we live were developed into shops, restaurants, a multi-screen cinema and . . . an indoor ski slope! You can perhaps imagine how intrigued I was about the ski slope, having been born in the midst of the French Alps, a region known for its ski resorts, whereas West Yorkshire is a place better known for mining! The only hills you see where we live are the slack heaps from the mines! They cannot compete with the height and beauty of the Alps. The other thing I wondered was, who on earth could have imagined that skiing would be popular here? However, the Frenchman who had the idea to build the ski slope saw the whole thing from a different angle. As far as he was concerned, he was about to create a desire to ski in the heart of Yorkshire! How? Simply by building a ski slope. Of course, once the locals tried it, they loved it and the desire to ski was sown. Now the place is always packed. You can buy skiing equipment there and you can take skiing lessons. It feels just like a genuine ski station. Simply amazing! But who would have thought it would work in an ex-mining town?

It is my conviction that the Lord operates in the same way as this enterprising Frenchman. He creates in us a desire for the things He wants us to do! Let me illustrate this from the Bible.

In Genesis we read that the Lord created Adam and then He said, *"It is not good for the man to be alone"* {Genesis 2:18).

God knew this before He said it, of course. It is not as if it had suddenly dawned on Him. God knew that it was not good for man to be alone, but at that point Adam didn't know it. He didn't know that he needed a wife. So how did the Lord make Adam realise it? He created in Adam the *need* for Eve. How? By summoning all the animals, male and female, so that Adam could name them. Adam named all the animals, but the Bible says that, *"for Adam **no suitable helper** was found"* (Genesis 2:20, emphasis added).

As Adam went through the process of naming all the animals, male and female, he soon realised that every male in creation had his female counterpart, every male, that is, except ... him! The desire was created in Adam by the Lord, and the Lord Himself answered it by creating Eve.

Some of the desires we have in our hearts come from the Lord Himself. Of course they need to be tested and maybe shared with those we can trust. It would be folly to trust every single desire that we have, because we could easily be misled by our feelings and emotions. However, let us not forget the fact that our desires can come from the Lord and when that is the case, He uses them to lead us to the path He wants us to walk. The Bible says in Proverbs 21:1 that,

> *"The king's heart is in the hand of the* Lord;
>   *he directs it like a watercourse wherever he pleases."*

Consider these verses also:

> *"Turn my heart towards your statutes*
> *and not towards selfish gain."*

(Psalm 119:36)

> *"In his heart a man plans his course,*
> *but the* Lord *determines his steps."*

(Proverbs 16:9)

Chapter 5

Moving from Shadow to Substance

The only way to move from the shadow to the substance is through Christ. Jesus is the only door to our salvation, the only door to our real identity and to the works He has prepared for us. Therefore, it is not possible to reach the substance of our lives except through the One by whom all things were created: things in heaven and on earth, visible and invisible, whether thrones or powers or rulers or authorities; all things were created by him and for him (Colossians 1:16). All over the world, millions of people are trying to find an answer for the desires created by the thought of eternity that the Lord breathed into all humanity through Adam. This signal within us is constantly trying to tune in to the divine transmitter, but it is muffled by all sorts of interference, leaving us feeling dissatisfied and empty. The soul then craves other things to satisfy itself and here begins a downward spiral. Through the cross however, Jesus brings us back to His purposes and clears the channels of communication so that we can hear His voice again. He reconciles us with our purpose in life.

Our life and identity is hidden with Christ in God along with the things He is calling us to do. To find Christ is to find oneself. To find Christ is to find the person you were created to be, the real "you", the one God saw before the creation of the world. To find Jesus is to find the bridge, the interface, the mediator between the shadow and the substance of yourself. When the the writer to the Hebrews compares the ministry of the Old Testament priests to the ministry of Jesus, he says:

> "But the ministry Jesus has received is as superior to theirs as the covenant of which he is **mediator** is superior to the old one, and it is founded on better promises."
>
> (Hebrews 8:6, emphasis added)

The Greek word for "mediator" is *mesites*, which means "one who intervenes between two, either to make or restore peace and friendship, or form a pact, or for ratifying a covenant". Jesus is our mediator! Through Him we make peace with God and have access to all the Father's promises. He brings the old and the new together. He is the mediator between the shadow and the substance. He is the bridge between the two – the One who says *"Follow me ... and I will make you ... "* (Matthew 4:19). "Follow Me," Jesus says, "and I will make you into the substance of what I want you to be."

To follow Jesus is to go somewhere! If we are not going anywhere, then we are not following Him. If we are not changing, not becoming more like Him every day, then we are not following Him. He is always on the move and He invites us to walk with Him. He is leading us to become the person He intends us to be – leading us from shadow to substance.

During the time of Jesus' ministry on earth, one man experienced a mighty encounter with the mediator, and his life was changed forever (Luke 5)! The man was a fisherman called Peter. One particular night he had worked without catching anything. I can imagine the scene: Peter is sitting with the other fishermen, repairing and cleaning their nets by the Lake of Galilee. None of his colleagues dare to speak to him because of his fiery temper. Tired and disappointed with the night's work he tries to console himself with the thought that tomorrow will be a better day. A good catch of fish would bring in enough money to pay for his fishing equipment and support his family. He notices a gathering of people not far from where they are sitting and recognises the one they call Jesus. He can hardly hear what is being said, but it doesn't matter because he is too busy working.

Maybe Peter thought that the crowd were wasting their time listening to this "preacher" and would be better off getting back to work and doing something useful? Maybe, for just a few moments, he would have loved to stop and listen to what Jesus was saying after vaguely hearing Him talking about a "kingdom that is like a fishing net".

"What does He know about fishing anyway!" Peter grumbled and returned to his work with a feeling of emptiness in his heart. This business of a "new kingdom coming to earth" was nothing new to him. He had heard people talking about it before and found himself believing that a better life was possible, But then he had to face the facts – it was not coming and it was even less likely with a foreign army occupying his hometown! He was despondent and empty.

The Bible tells us that there were two boats left at the water's edge and one belonged to Peter. His boat, motionless and still dirty after a night out at sea was a good picture of Peter's life. It was going nowhere. His life desperately needed direction, a map, a good compass and a good captain. Jesus saw the two

empty boats as an opportunity to step into Peter's life. The Lord
cannot help but notice "empty boats" – empty lives left drifting,
crying out for better shores. He knows the desires of our hearts!
He is the One who puts certain desires there in the first place.

Jesus wanted to teach the people from one of the boats, so He
stepped into Peter's (knowing perfectly well whose boat it was!)
and asked him to put out a little from the shore. The Lord was
taking Peter symbolically away from the shores of his life and
drawing him little by little, ever so gently into something better.
I believe Peter was being led into the substance of his life.
Remember, he was encountering the mediator! He was now
"forced" to listen to the Master's teaching, since he was alone
with Him in a boat and some distance from shore.

I imagine Peter using the oars from time to time to keep the
boat parallel to the shore for Jesus. What was Jesus teaching
the crowd? Was He talking about the kingdom of God being like
a fishing net? Was He challenging the people to believe, to have
faith in God and not to fear tomorrow, to not worry about
having enough food or clothes? Or was He inviting them to love
one another and even to love their enemies? One thing I am sure
about is that He was not talking only to the crowd. The man in
the boat with Him was listening to every word; a man unable to
run away. Each word Jesus spoke was like a knife in his heart.
Jesus didn't need to look at Peter. He knew that this fisherman
was being shaken to the core by what was happening and by
what he was hearing. Peter was probably relieved when Jesus
finished speaking and he could start rowing back to shore, but
the Lord had not finished with him yet. He wanted to take him
into an even deeper revelation, much deeper than anything He
had said to the crowd. He had something especially for Peter,
something that would take him into a much deeper understanding of the purposes of God for his life.

"Put out into deep water and let down the nets for a catch" said Jesus (Luke 5:4). Peter stopped and looked at Jesus in disbelief. *"... we've worked hard all night and haven't caught anything ..."* (Luke 5:5) he answered, trying to avoid going back out to face the same failure again. Jesus was not put off by him, so Peter did as he was asked and said: *"... because you say so, I will let down the nets"* (Luke 5:5). The Bible says that when they had done so, they caught such a large number of fish that their nets began to break. When Peter saw this, he fell at Jesus' feet and said, *"Go away from me, Lord; I am a sinful man!"* (Luke 5:8). He and all his companions were astonished at the enormous catch of fish they had taken; so were James and John, the sons of Zebedee, Peter's partners.

Peter felt the guilt of his unbelief. He had thought he was going to give the preacher a fishing lesson he would never forget, maybe hoping that Jesus would fail to catch any fish, just like him the night before? This would have reassured him that he was not the only one who could fail and that he was still a good fisherman after all. How interesting! It is often when we feel at the end of ourselves, unsure about the things we were so good at before, that God can use us. Then Jesus said something amazing to Peter. He said, *"Don't be afraid; from now on you will catch men"* (Luke 5:10).

Jesus showed Peter what was the substance of his life. No longer would he live in the shadow; he was no longer a fisherman but a fisher-of-men. His shadow had the same shape as his substance – he was fishing – but he was meant to be catching men, not fish! Jesus, the mediator, brought the two together.

For Peter the implications were that he had to leave his job. Not all of us have to do this in order to follow Jesus, but we are all called to live a life that He has prepared for us. Jesus is still doing today what He did for Peter. All over the world He is still taking people from shadow to substance. He did it for me fourteen years ago and He wants to do it for you today! Peter and his fellow workers pulled their boats up on to shore, left everything and followed Him. Notice that the Bible says that they left *everything*. We will come back to this statement later.

In Luke 5:6 we see an interesting statement. It says,

> " . . . *they caught such a large number of fish that their nets began to break.*"

I believe the Bible is indicating here that when Peter first encountered Jesus and was told he would become a fisher of men, he was not yet ready. On one level, the fact that the nets were beginning to break as a vast number of fish flooded in, could be interpreted as signifying God's amazing, abundant provision. But on another level I believe it is symbolic of the fact that Peter was fragile and far from ready to attain the substance of his higher calling. He needed to undergo the Master's training before he would be ready to "contain" God's call on his life without breaking.

Three years later in John 21:6, Peter found himself in virtually the same situation, having been out at sea all night without success. Again he followed Jesus' instructions and a huge haul of fish followed, but this time the nets did not break! This time, I believe, Peter was ready to be a fisher of men. The only problem was, he had returned to his job as a fisherman; he had returned to the shadow instead of living in the substance. This is why the Lord shouted to him from the shore and told Peter to throw his net on the other side of the boat – symbolically inviting him not to go back to the life of a fisherman (shadow) but to live in the substance – his life was on the other side!

When Peter eventually became a fisher of men he knew plenty of "tricks" he could use to catch them; techniques he had learned as a fisherman that he used when he became the great apostle to the Jews. Here is food for thought that will help us to consider how to draw parallels between our own shadow and substance.

It was Jesus Himself in Matthew 13:47 that said the kingdom of heaven is like a net that was let down into a lake and caught all kinds of fish. It would not have been difficult for Peter to imagine a net full of different kinds of fish. Different kinds of fish means exactly that! Different sizes, shapes, colours and tastes.

Fishing nets were not generally calibrated to catch only one kind of fish, but many. When Jesus died on the cross, He re-calibrated the net of the kingdom of heaven to open it up to all humanity, not exclusively the Jews. What a relief that the kingdom of heaven is open to us all! It is like a kaleidoscope of differences and the Lord takes pleasure in looking at it. Unfortunately we are not all like this, we often prefer to mix with our own kind of people.

As a young Christian I made the decision to live in a Christian community. We all lived together on a farm and we shared everything. Everything was going just fine until the leaders decided to let a tramp move in with us! The man was definitely searching for God, but was still struggling with alcohol and anger. One day the police called us to say he was drunk in the middle of town and asked us to go and pick him up. I went to get him and put him in the back seat of my lovely new car. He was drunk and angry and kept shouting at me and kicking the car door. Then he started vomiting in the car and kicked the back window so violently that he smashed it to pieces! I was so angry! I wanted to leave him by the side of the road. He was not my kind of person. He was not the kind of fish I liked! But the kingdom of heaven is a net that is loving and without discrimination! Even these kinds of fish do not manage to escape the net of God's love for humanity.

Peter knew that nets bring back all kinds of different fish and he was forcefully reminded of this when the Lord showed him a vision of a large sheet being let down from heaven by its four corners, coming down to where he was (Acts 11:5). In the vision he was shown certain impure animals and was told to kill and eat them. He refused, but was instructed twice not to call anything impure that God had made clean. Jesus' work on the cross re-calibrated the net of salvation so that it could bring back Gentile as well as Jewish "fish". Immediately after this vision, the fish Cornelius was caught! Peter told the brothers in Jerusalem everything and came to this conclusion:

> "I now realise how true it is that God does not show favouritism but accepts men from every nation who fear him and do what is right."

(Acts 10:34–35)

Thank God for his mercy towards us!

Three ways of catching fish

There are three basic ways of catching fish that Peter could have employed which will give us further insight:

1. Letting down the nets

This was done by using two boats and was probably the way Peter was fishing with his companions when he met Jesus in

Luke 5. The net was tied between two boats at the rear and was let down between them. The net hung vertically in the water because of weights attached to the bottom and floats attached along the top edge. The two rowing boats would then move forward, dragging the net and creating a sort of a cone which would trap the fish. This technique required two boats and several men to haul up the net full of fish.

This was the shadow of things to come for Peter. His impulsive nature meant he would sometimes need another "boat" in order to help him let down his net and be an effective fisher of men. The Lord provided another boat for Peter by putting John alongside him. Peter and John were very different in both personality and character. Peter was impulsive, John was more meditative. Jesus knew this and so we find them working together sometimes, in the beginning of the book of Acts for example, as fishers of men.

2. Throwing the net

This is the technique Peter and the other disciples used in John 21. The net was thrown out from the boat (or sometimes from the shore) and then dragged back. It is a good illustration of Peter's ministry as an evangelist at Pentecost in Acts 2:14–17. He threw the net of the gospel by raising his voice and addressing the crowd. The result of this catch of fish is seen in verse 41. When he pulled the net back in, those who accepted his message were baptised and about three thousand were added to their number that day.

3. Throwing out a line

Using a simple line and hook with bait, this was a one man method to catch fish one at a time. This was the way of fishing suggested by Jesus in Matthew 17:27:

> *" ... go to the lake and throw out your line. Take the first fish*
> *you catch; open its mouth and you will find a four-drachma*
> *coin ... "*

Some of the fish we might be called to catch are to be caught on
a one-to-one basis. They are special fish, people of influence, like
Jesus said, they have gold in their mouths. They would not
necessarily come to our church meetings; you need to go after
them. It could be your boss, your director, your line manager.
They do not come easily. This is the kind of fish Cornelius was
for Peter. Cornelius was an important man, a centurion in what
was known as the Italian Regiment. It would have been
impossible for Cornelius to enter a synagogue, yet here was a
man who would influence a great deal of people through his
conversion. The only way to catch him was to throw a single
line.

Listening to the man standing on the shore

In John 21, the disciples were fishing unsuccessfully yet again. A
man was standing on the shore and was calling out to them to
throw their net on the other side of the boat. They did not
know it was Jesus. In Galilee, the sun is sometimes so bright
that one man from a fishing team would stay on the shore to
have a better visibility of the water. He would look over the
water from a different angle without being blinded by the sun,
so that he could clearly see where the fish were and inform his
team.

In the same way Peter had to be sensitive to the voice of
God's Spirit telling him where to cast his net; where to throw his
line; where the fish were! This is a good reminder for us that we
need to hear the prophetic voice of God so that we will always

be sensitive to His leading. His commission will not change, we will always have to go and make disciples of all the nations, but where we do it and how we do it is very important. We do not want to be repeating things simply because they worked yesterday. The world has changed, our message has not, but the way in which we convey it needs to. In a world saturated by information and all kinds of technology, we need to hear the voice of the Lord calling out from the shore and telling us where and how to throw the net!

Peter himself is a vivid example of this. After his vision of the sheet coming down from heaven, foreshadowing the gospel being preached to the Gentiles, Peter could have declared himself the "apostle to the Gentiles" don't you think? He declared in Acts 15:7,

> *"Brothers, you know that some time ago God made a choice among you that the Gentiles might hear from my lips the message of the gospel and believe."*

He could have concluded that because he was the one who had the vision from God about preaching the gospel to the Gentiles, there was no reason to think that he should not carry on catching Gentile fish. But both Peter and Paul heard the voice of the Spirit, the voice from "the shore" telling them where their individual work (substance) was to be done. The apostle Paul said in Galatians 2:7–8,

> *"... they saw that I had been entrusted with the task of preaching the gospel to the Gentiles, just as Peter had been to the Jews. For God, who was at work in the ministry of Peter as an apostle to the Jews, was also at work in my ministry as an apostle to the Gentiles."*

Naturally, both of them could have come to the wrong conclusion concerning their ministry. That is why in the context of our theme "the shadow of the things to come", we need to be very careful not to jump to obvious *natural* conclusions, but listen for the voice of the One calling out from the shore!

After fishing

After fishing, nets were washed, dried and repaired on the shore. Peter, like any other fisherman, knew how important it was to look after his fishing nets. They are the fisherman's most important tool. If the net is not properly cared for it will not last. If it is not repaired after use then the broken threads will leave too big a gap and small fish will escape.

I am not alone in feeling alarmed at the fact that less and less people are attracted by the teaching of the Word, and more and more are running after conceptual truths that are not building the Church. Some churches are just keeping Christians occupied with navel gazing and have exchanged the God of the Bible for a father Christmas figure with his hands full of presents.

If the fishing net is a picture of the kingdom of God, then we need to watch over our doctrine and our foundations very carefully, not allowing gaps of "conformity" (to the pattern of this world) to develop. Lowering standards in order to catch more fish, or allowing the fish to feel "entertained" at church is, I believe, a very dangerous game which is starting to backfire on Western nations. I would agree that we need to change the vehicle, but *not* the message. The price to pay is a whole generation not entering into the substance of what the Lord has prepared. Let us revisit our nets, our foundations, and make sure we sew and repair the net where it is needed so that we can leave a legacy that is worth all that our fathers in the faith have worked for.

Chapter 6

Why is it So Important to Move into the Substance?

A crucial reason for pursuing the substance of our lives is that we begin to be fruitful in the kingdom of God when we leave the shadow. Peter became a great apostle when he left his fishing business. He became a man of great influence and left an eternal deposit in all those he encountered.

For him, moving into the substance meant he had to leave everything behind. Not all of us are called to leave our jobs (something we will explore further in the next chapter). It is a question of being where God wants us to be.

In the parable of the talents (Matthew 25:14) there is a very important principle that is often missed. We tend to restrict the meaning of the parable to the importance of multiplying the deposit the Lord has invested in us, but we often fail to understand what sort of multiplication He means and how to go about it.

Let's look more closely at the parable and see what we can learn from it.

> *"Again, [the kingdom] will be like a man going on a journey,*
> *who called his servants and entrusted his property to them. To*
> *one he gave five talents of money, to another two talents, and to*
> *another one talent, each according to his ability. Then he went on*
> *his journey."*
>
> (Matthew 25:14–15)

It is very important to notice the phrase, "each one according to his ability". The gifts and potential the Lord places in us are given according to our ability. We will not be able to say that we were given too much or too little. It was given *according* to our ability. Your ability is different from others; you cannot compare yourself with your brother or sister in Christ. They received their share according to their ability. The only possible competition you can feel is between you and yourself – what you *could have done* with your share and what you *have done* with it. This is why reaching the substance is so important. The "substance" is your maximum ability and potential in Christ.

> *"The man who had received the five talents went at once and put*
> *his money to work and gained five more. So also, the one with the*
> *two talents gained two more. But the man who had received*
> *the one talent went off, dug a hole in the ground and hid his*
> *master's money."*
>
> (Matthew 25:16–18)

This was the way some people in Jesus' day kept their money safe from thieves. They dug a hole in the ground and buried their possessions!

> *"After a long time the master of those servants returned and*
> *settled accounts with them. The man who had received the five*

talents brought the other five. 'Master,' he said, 'you entrusted
me with five talents. See, I have gained five more.'

His master replied, 'Well done, good and faithful servant! You
have been faithful with a few things; I will put you in charge of
many things. Come and share your master's happiness!'

The man with the two talents also came. 'Master,' he said,
'you entrusted me with two talents; see, I have gained two
more.'

His master replied, 'Well done, good and faithful servant! You
have been faithful with a few things; I will put you in charge of
many things. Come and share your master's happiness!'

Then the man who had received the one talent came. 'Master,'
he said, 'I knew that you are a hard man, harvesting where you
have not sown and gathering where you have not scattered seed.
So I was afraid and went out and hid your talent in the ground.
See, here is what belongs to you.'"

(Matthew 25:19–25)

Was the servant afraid of the master? Was he afraid to lose
what he had, that someone might steal what he had been
entrusted with? Or was he just looking for a pitiful excuse for his
laziness?

"His master replied, 'You wicked, lazy servant! So you knew that
I harvest where I have not sown and gather where I have not
scattered seed?'"

(Matthew 25:26)

It is interesting to notice that the master does not contradict the
last part of his servant's statement, but uses it against him: *"So
you knew that I harvest where I have not sown and gather where I have
not scattered seed?"*

The only thing he does not reiterate is, "*... you are a hard man ...*", but he repeats the rest to reinforce the truth of the way Jesus operates. This is how the master in the story is and how he settles accounts! It seems very unfair don't you think? How can the master gather and harvest where he has not scattered and sown? Is this possible? How can a farmer harvest in a field where he has not sown and then complain about the poor results? But we know the Lord is always fair, so something must be hidden. What does the master mean?

The talents invested in your life are there so that you can also bless others. Let us think about it in terms of "seed and fields" as in the parable. The talents given to the three men are the seed. Symbolically they are the gifts given to us by our Father in heaven. They are not our possessions, they are His and He has entrusted us with them.

You are doing the Master's will when you multiply His investment and sow these seeds in fields of opportunity presented to you during your time on earth. These fields are the lives of people who cross your path, encounters ordained by the "divine farmer". When you sow seed (your gifts) into someone's field (life), his field has *your* seed planted in it, ready to burst into life and bear fruit in season. When the Master returns to gather the harvest in that person's life, He will find a harvest produced by seed sown by you! So, the Master comes and gathers a harvest He has sown through you. This is how He can say that He harvests where He has not sown and gathers where He has not scattered seed.

So, some of the seed God gives to you is to be sown and hopefully the recipient will do the same! By doing so, you are faithfully multiplying the gifts given to you. Here begins a chain of imparted gifts that runs through generations. When Judgment Day comes and the Master "settles the accounts", He will expect a harvest produced from your seed to be found in the lives of those He presented to you as opportunities during your lifetime. Obviously the success of the harvest also depends on the faithfulness of the one who receives your seed, but you must be sure to do your part of the job.

I was head of percussion in the Conservatoire National de Region de Grenoble for eleven years, and in my first year I was blessed with some very gifted and enthusiastic students. They have gone on to teach in some of the most prominent music academies in France and play for symphonic orchestras. A few years ago I was invited by Christophe, one of these students, to be on a panel of judges for the graduation exam of some of the most advanced percussionists in his class. I examined gifted musicians for the whole day and was amazed to notice certain characteristics in the way that they played that I would claim as my own. The reason for this phenomena was that Christophe, their teacher and my former student, had been influenced by me as I taught him and had in turn influenced his students with that same seed. I could see my style of playing in Christophe's students; my seed in his students! Three generations have been influenced by the precious deposit certain great musicians planted in my life. Something of them was sown in me and I have in turn passed it on to others, like passing on the baton in a relay race. This is a good illustration of what the Master expects of us. He will come back and harvest where He has not sown, expecting to find the harvest of what other people have sown in my life, and equally expecting to find in others a harvest from the seed I was given to sow.

At all costs we should avoid following the path of the "lazy" servant. Bible expositor John Gill, writing about the servant who buried the one talent he was given, made the following observations in his commentary on Matthew:

"He neglected the gift that was in him, he made no use of it, either to his own advantage, or to the good of others, and the interest of his Lord; he either never went into the ministry, or if he did, he left it as Demas did, having too great affection for the world, and the things of it: he minded earth and earthly things, and employed himself in them, and not in his master's work and service. The phrase seems to point out the earthly mindedness of the man, his worldly disposition, and his eager pursuit after the things of life; which were the reason why he disregarded his talent, and made no use of his ministerial gifts: he could not deny worldly self, nor leave all to follow Christ; but rather than drop the world, he chose to bury his talent in it: it was his Lord's money and not his own, and he was accountable to him for it, and should have used it in another manner."[1]

In Jesus' parable, what was the reaction of the master to his servant? After scolding him for being wicked and lazy, the master continues saying,

> *"Well then, you should have put my money on deposit with the bankers, so that when I returned I would have received it back with interest."*
>
> (Matthew 25:27)

The servant made two big mistakes when he buried the talent. Firstly, he did not try to multiply it by investing it and secondly, if he wasn't going to put the talent to work, then he should have deposited the money in the bank so he would at least have received a small amount of interest to show his master an increase. In the context of using our talents, "bankers" are those who help us develop and increase our gifts. We will touch on the subject of sharpening one's gift in the following chapter.

We find Paul teaching the same principle of sowing the seed invested in us in 2 Corinthians 9:10:

> *"Now he who supplies seed to the sower and bread for food will also supply and increase your store of seed and will enlarge the harvest of your righteousness."*

The context of this passage is "giving" and does not only apply to money. The apostle Paul distinguishes "seed" from bread. He clearly says that seed is for the sower and bread is for food, and that both are supplied by the Lord. Everything we receive from God is to serve two purposes: to sow into others or for us to eat. The problem is that we tend to eat the seed as well as the bread! We eat the portion we should be sowing in others. Paul urges the church in Corinth to live according to this divine law. The more you are prepared to sow, the more the Lord will increase your store of seed. He will provide the bread to eat! He will provide for the mortgage, the car, the university fees etc.

The same applies in the parable of the talents. Those who are gifted are expected to sow some of their provision into other people's lives. If you stay in the shadow and don't move into the substance you are effectively burying your gift, or using it only for yourself. As a fisherman Peter must have passed on some of his expertise and experience to his colleagues. You could say he sowed his seed into their lives. However, if you compare the kind of seed he was sharing before and after his encounter with Jesus in Luke 5, it is clear that Peter was having an eternal impact living in the substance of what Christ had prepared for him, even while he was still a fisherman.

Of course you can sow into others' lives when you are in the shadow, but you will fall short of the complete "vineyard" of God's will for your life and you will not have the opportunity of sowing your seed in the fields the Lord provides for you. Basically, you are just a "shadow" of what you could be. You might develop your gifts (and we will see how important that is), you may earn a living using them, but there is so much more that can be done with the gifts the Lord has entrusted you with. Peter could have remained a "gifted fisherman", but he became a gifted fisher of men and changed thousands of lives as a result.

One day, all of us will be left with just one talent – the gift of experience – and we cannot permit ourselves to bury it. If we are gifted musically, or in sport, or business, these things run a natural course in life. Usually we cannot keep using this talent until the day we die. But the ultimate talent of experience should never be buried. What a waste to hear older people concede defeat, saying that "their time" is over "let the younger ones do it", instead of sharing from their wealth of experience and warning the younger generation of the mistakes that should be avoided. Our God is a multi-generational God, the God of Abraham, Isaac and Jacob! The Bible strongly emphasises the necessity of teaching the next generation. There is a serious lack of "grey hair" in the charismatic movement of today.

How have I been fully known?

Another good reason to move into the substance is because there you become what you are truly meant to be. In the substance you are doing the things you were born to do with the gifts that God has blessed you with. It is said that there is a duality in all of us: the person you are, and the person you think you are. It is a tragedy when people spend all their time trying to develop the person they think they are, whilst neglecting the person they really are.

Living in the substance is becoming the person Christ wants you to be. We live in a world where people are known more by what they do than who they are, but Jesus reverses this humanistic equation by inviting you to become the one He wants you to be, so that you will do the things He wants you to do. Moving into the substance is becoming the one God saw before the foundation of the world. The apostle Paul talks to the Corinthians about a time when perfection will do away with partial revelation, and says this:

> *"For now we see in a mirror dimly, but then face to face; now I know in part; then I shall know fully, even as I am fully known."*
> (1 Corinthians 13:12)

At present, we see ourselves and the mysteries of God through a dimmed mirror and we have a partial, imperfect understanding of the things yet to come. One day, however, says the apostle Paul, our sight will be perfect; the view will be full and clear without the least obstruction and we will see ourselves, fully known by God. We will see the kind of person He saw when He looked at us before the foundation of the world. I wonder how much difference there is between what we are and what we could have been? I have been fully known says the apostle. I was known by God before I was born; I was known by God in all the potential I could achieve; God saw me in the substance. On that glorious day the Bible also says that I will know Him; I will know the substance He had planned for me and He will measure the difference between the two.

A revelation of our true self is found today in Christ. He is the substance of Jacob's ladder, a staircase resting on the earth with its top reaching to heaven. He was the One who prayed *"Your will be done on earth as it is in heaven"* (Matthew 6:10). You are hidden in Him (Colossians 3) and seated with Him in the heavenlies (Ephesians 2:6). I wonder if there is a "virtual model" of us all in heaven?! By "model" I mean the potential perfect spiritual me in Christ, the heavenly Gabriel in Jesus' mind, seen before the world was created – not a real being of course, but the thought in God that knows who I am at my full spiritual potential. Is it possible that the image of me in Christ, when projected from heaven could create a shadow on earth just like the heavenly sanctuary did? Does this mean that on earth I am constantly moving into the substance of my life, being changed from glory into glory? I can't say. We see in a mirror dimly, we know in part, but one day it will become clear! What I do know is that the Lord knows who I am now and He knows the heavenly being He wants me to become. Paul was the only one that had a revelation of this and he writes in 2 Corinthians 12:1–4:

> *" . . . I will go on to visions and revelations from the Lord. I know a man in Christ who fourteen years ago was caught up to the third heaven. Whether it was in the body or out of the body I do not know – God knows. And I know that this man – whether in the body or apart from the body I do not know, but God knows – was caught up to paradise. He heard inexpressible things, things that man is not permitted to tell."*

Paul is talking about himself in this passage – the "man in Christ". John Gill writes in his commentary,

> "Whether Paul was caught up to the third heaven as John was 'in the Spirit' on the Lord's day, and Ezekiel was taken by a lock of his head, and lifted up by the Spirit between

earth and heaven, and brought 'in the visions of God to Jerusalem', cannot be said. The apostle did not know himself, and much less can any other be able to say how it was; it is best with him to refer and leave it to the omniscient God; he knew not where he was, or whether in the body or out."

The most important thing to remember is that when you are in the substance you are the one Christ wants you to be and you do the things He wants you to do with the gifts He has given you. When you are what you are supposed to be, you do what you are supposed to do! When you are in the substance you become a greater source of influence. In the substance you can sow seeds of eternal value into the fields you pass through during your pilgrimage on earth. Jesus is still saying to those who are listening, "Come follow Me and I will make you the best of who you can be. I am taking you from the shadow to the substance of all that I have for you and you will be a great source of encouragement and blessing to all those who cross your path."

In the substance you align yourself with the perfect will of God. You may want to pause now and pray this simple prayer:

"Jesus, You are the way, the door to the substance of who I really am in You. I want to follow You and let You help me to become the one I was meant to be and do the things I was born to do."

If you are reading this book and you do not know Jesus, you need to realise that He has given you a life, a purpose and gifts so that you can fulfil the works you came into this world to do. It is only through Jesus and His sacrifice on the cross for your sins that you can discover His plans for you. You need to ask for and receive His forgiveness for your sins and for all the things that you have done against His will. Come out of darkness into His wonderful light and from there you will see the shadow and be able to move into the substance of your life.

Note

1. John Gill's Exposition of the Whole Bible, www.freegrace.net/gill/, public domain.

Chapter 7

Things to Consider When Moving from the Shadow to the Substance

It does not necessarily mean leaving your job

Not all of us are called to leave our secular jobs in order to fulfil God's calling on our lives. For many their secular jobs *are* their calling. Both scenarios are fine, it all depends on what God is asking you to do.

Peter left the fishing business in response to Jesus' challenge to him. When the prophet Elisha was called to become Elijah's successor (1 Kings 19:21), he took his yoke of oxen and slaughtered them. He burned the ploughing equipment to cook the meat before following Elijah and becoming his attendant. He left everything to follow Elijah, in fact he even burned his farming equipment, but again, not all the people who had an encounter with the Lord were called to leave their jobs and follow Him. In some instances Jesus very specifically asked them to return to where they came from so that they could be a good testimony there doing their job. I know many people with full-time jobs who are living in the substance because of their employment. They have understood the equation between the shadow and the substance and have put it into practice daily.

At our church we have a team of leaders rather than a single pastor. My brother-in-law, Phil, is one of the team. He is an engineer and a manager by profession. He leads a large team of employees and carries huge responsibilities in the important decisions he makes. Some of these decisions have enormous financial implications on the company he works for. He is a leader in his job and a leader at church. As a Spirit-filled Christian he uses the same gifts of leading and managing in his job and at church. He understands group dynamics and can therefore anticipate tensions between members of a team. He knows who would work together best and why. He also knows which combinations to avoid in the same team. This is a wonderful asset for our church, but Phil recognises that if he left his job now, he would lose some of his sharpness in leading teams of people and in bearing the weight of eldership in the body of Christ. It does not change the fact that he is living in the substance and not in the shadow.

Maybe a time will come when the Lord will call Phil out of his job, but let us not reduce living in the substance to "full-time ministry in the church". It is a matter of being sensitive to what God wants for us so that we can follow His plan and become what He wants us to be. This is the real understanding of living in the substance. Many Christians with secular jobs are actually in full-time ministry by the very nature of what they do. Each one of us has to hear God for himself and live in close accountability with one another so that nothing is done in a hurry, but rather wisely for the benefit of the kingdom of God. Leaving the shadow and moving into the substance means I understand the dynamics between the two and how the gifts can be used in both domains.

How and where can I sharpen my gifts?

In order to have something to offer in the substance we need to develop our gifts to their full capacity. Remember that what we do with our talents is one of the criteria for Jesus' judgment (Matthew 25). As we discovered earlier, the lazy servant made two crucial mistakes:

1.   He did not increase the capital entrusted to him.
2.   He did not sow into others.

The master in Jesus' story said to his servant, "You should have put my money on deposit with the bankers ..." This would have been a good start and better than doing nothing. Failing in this meant he had little chance of fulfilling the second requirement. A banker's role is to keep our money safe, but also to increase the sum of money we have invested, if we are prepared to leave it there for a little while. So then, who are these bankers and how can they increase our capital? Proverbs 27:17 says,

> *"As iron sharpens iron,*
> *so one man sharpens another."*

Note that the Bible doesn't say "as stone sharpens iron" (even though it would work to some extent) or "as iron sharpens wood" (again possible!). Rather it says "as iron sharpens iron". In other words, the same material is used to sharpen itself. I believe there is an important key for us here that could unlock our understanding about the bankers: the best way to sharpen our gift is to find the same gift (iron versus iron), but sharper.

Too often I have met desperate and frustrated Christian artists who are trying to sharpen their gift by rubbing against a totally different one! Of course we can learn something from everyone and I would always encourage people to get a variety of input from a variety of different sources, but still I am convinced that the best results are achieved when both gifts are the same. For example, a drummer will be sharpened most effectively by a better drummer. A prophet will develop his gift by spending time with God of course, but also by learning from another prophet with more experience than he has. The examples could go on forever. Think about your gift and apply this principle.

I believe you can even go to an unbeliever to be sharpened, since most invest all their time in working on their gifts! Many people live for nothing else other than their primary gift. For them it is all that counts in life and they tend to be very sharp because they have invested years developing their gift at the expense of everything else. They have a wealth of experience that you could do with! A good example is a vocal coach for instance. If your gift is singing and you want to serve the Lord using your voice in worship, then you should seek out the very best vocal teacher and study with them. It may well be that the best vocal coach in your town is an unbeliever.

Some churches teach that you should not go into the "world" – to "Egypt" as it were – to hone your gift, but rather learn from God and from the community of believers only. But I would disagree with that view apart from certain exceptions; for instance if you are learning from someone who is involved in any spiritual activity contrary to the Bible. Churches that teach this kind of self-sufficiency have developed a level of mediocrity that has resulted in ridiculous comments like, "Don't worry if you can't sing in tune, because God hears you in tune!" How stupid! Of course that's not true. God has perfect pitch, and He, unlike the rest of the band and congregation, forgives you!

Even worse are those who believe that any involvement with the arts should be abandoned the minute you become a Christian. Effectively they make the artist into a pastor instead and therefore separate that person from the "world" (a world that we are supposed to reach?). The result is a bunch of frustrated and miserable people, the "pastors" and their flocks. Art is a gift from God to the Church and like any other gift, it needs developing to its full potential.

Moses was educated in Egypt and he learned to be a leader in Egyptian society. He was trained to a very high level in Egypt. God dealt with Moses' character later on in the desert, then he was equipped and ready to fulfil his calling.

Before we move towards the substance of our lives we must make sure that we have developed and sharpened our gifts. The majority of us have several gifts and not just one. All of them need sharpening to their full potential, according to our capacity. Let me share a personal example of what happened to me when I went off in search of some "iron" to sharpen me!

As a young musician, after finishing my music degrees I decided to move to New York, knowing that I would find the most talented and sharpened musicians there. One of my students had given me the phone number of a saxophonist friend of his who worked with some of the finest musicians in the city. I took the bull by the horns and rang him and shortly it was arranged that I would go to New York and stay with him for a while.

I will never forget the feeling of arriving at JFK airport and jumping into a big yellow cab. I gave the driver a piece of paper with the address where I was going and as we drove through Manhattan my heart felt like it would explode. Thoughts were rushing through my mind "This is it," I thought. "This is what I have been waiting for; this is what I have been dreaming of!" When we reached the address, Rolando, my host, was waiting for me and wanted to know what I was looking for in New York. We chatted and after breakfast the next day, he opened a little phone book containing the numbers of some of the best drummers in the world. I recognised many names as my heroes and could not believe I had the chance of meeting them. A sense of panic hit me when he asked me to choose one! I chose Billy Hart, one of the finest jazz drummers in the world. Rolando rang him and less than an hour later he was standing in front of me asking me what I thought of New York! In my broken English I babbled a few words, trying to calm down and not show any emotion, even though my legs were trembling at the thought of playing the drums in front of him. I sat in the back seat of his huge car with Billy driving and Rolando sat in the front next to him. Billy looked at me in the rear view mirror and after smiling at me, asked if I knew a particular jazz standard and if I would sing it to him.

For a few seconds I thought he was joking. "I'm a drummer, not a singer!" I said nervously.

"You can't play what you can't sing!" Billy said emphatically.

"OK, then . . ." I said, secretly thinking, "What am I doing here? Oh well, it's too late to bottle out now!"

In fact Billy was already beginning to sharpen my gift and we hadn't even gotten near a drum kit yet! I began to sing the standard, but he interrupted me saying, "There is not a lot of swing in the way you sing it. Can you give me more groove please?" At that point I knew I was in trouble; I knew it was make or break. He was either going to smash my gift up into little pieces or sharpen it like never before. It was all about attitude and determination and I realised I was about to need a great deal of both.

When we arrived at his place, to my horror I saw two drum kits facing one another. He sat behind one kit and invited me to use the other. He told me that he would play a few bars, then it was my turn. When he started playing I could hardly believe what I was seeing and hearing. He made the drums talk; he was one with them; everything about what he was doing was a delight to look at and to listen to. It seemed that he was born to play. When my turn came I must have looked like a geriatric bear and sounded like the guns of Navarone! He just smiled and carried on. He was the gazelle and I was the bear! This time he showed me even more skill and displayed the whole panopoly of drum vocabulary. Never mind sharpening my iron, he was breaking, melting and reshaping it.

"Next time it's my turn," I thought, "I have got to give it everything. This is the reason I came here. Come on, come on ... two, three, four ... "

I gave it everything I had and I noticed a change in my playing. My iron was becoming sharper. Something from him was in me! He stopped, looked me straight in the eye and said, "Great drumming Gabriel!"

You know what? I felt like I was floating on air. What an amazing feeling, what a joy. I had passed the first test of being sharpened by an iron like me, but much more experienced. The price to pay was the pain barrier and the humility needed to accept how much more needed to be achieved. This process needs to be seriously considered in our churches and maybe it is time for leaders to look at their people, identify their gifts and invest in them by sending them to those who can sharpen their gifts.

Failure and discouragement can tempt us to move back into the shadow

We have all found ourselves at some point being harassed by discouragement and weariness. I have been warned more than once that ministry is very difficult and that people can be extremely ungrateful and hard. A lot is expected from a preacher, a pastor or any other public ministry for that matter. Many have fallen into the temptation of creating an "atmosphere" in a meeting simply because that is what people want. Some Christians think that being in God's presence is the "experience" they have when music carries them into a soulish realm. People like these are bound to feel discouraged and disappointed sooner or later. We have a lot to answer for in what we have made our corporate "worship" into. The Lord is bringing about a reformation of worship that I am very excited about.

Some people feel they have failed God by falling short of His expectations. Others have realised that ministry is all about perseverance, endurance and a lot of hard work often dealing with difficult people. These kinds of discouragement tempt us to go back into the shadow.

In the gospel of John, chapter 21, Peter is discouraged and is faced with a decision. After three years of intense training and having tasted what it is like to be a fisher of men, he finds himself back at square one. Three years after his first encounter with Jesus in Luke 5, he is back in exactly the same situation, having denied Jesus three times in His time of need. We looked at this story in an earlier chapter, but now let us look at it from a different angle.

> *"Afterwards Jesus appeared again to his disciples, by the Sea of Tiberias. It happened this way: Simon Peter, Thomas (called Didymus), Nathanael from Cana in Galilee, the sons of Zebedee, and two other disciples were together. 'I'm going out to fish,' Simon Peter told them, and they said, 'We'll go with you.' So they went out and got into the boat, but that night they caught nothing.*

Early in the morning, Jesus stood on the shore, but the disciples did not realize that it was Jesus.

He called out to them, 'Friends, haven't you any fish?'

'No,' they answered.

He said, 'Throw your net on the right side of the boat and you will find some.' When they did, they were unable to haul the net in because of the large number of fish.

Then the disciple whom Jesus loved said to Peter, 'It is the Lord!' As soon as Simon Peter heard him say, 'It is the Lord,' he wrapped his outer garment around him (for he had taken it off) and jumped into the water. The other disciples followed in the boat, towing the net full of fish, for they were not far from shore, about a hundred yards. When they landed, they saw a fire of burning coals there with fish on it, and some bread.

Jesus said to them, 'Bring some of the fish you have just caught.'

Simon Peter climbed aboard and dragged the net ashore. It was full of large fish, 153, but even with so many the net was not torn. Jesus said to them, 'Come and have breakfast.' None of the disciples dared ask him, 'Who are you?' They knew it was the Lord. Jesus came, took the bread and gave it to them, and did the same with the fish. This was now the third time Jesus appeared to his disciples after he was raised from the dead.

When they had finished eating, Jesus said to Simon Peter, 'Simon son of John, do you truly love me more than these?'

'Yes, Lord,' he said, 'you know that I love you.'

Jesus said, 'Feed my lambs.'

Again Jesus said, 'Simon son of John, do you truly love me?'

He answered, 'Yes, Lord, you know that I love you.'

Jesus said, 'Take care of my sheep.'

The third time he said to him, 'Simon son of John, do you love me?'

> *Peter was hurt because Jesus asked him the third time, 'Do you love me?' He said, 'Lord, you know all things; you know that I love you.'*
>
> *Jesus said, 'Feed my sheep. I tell you the truth, when you were younger you dressed yourself and went where you wanted; but when you are old you will stretch out your hands, and someone else will dress you and lead you where you do not want to go.' Jesus said this to indicate the kind of death by which Peter would glorify God. Then he said to him, 'Follow me!' "*
>
> (John 21:1–19)

A despondent and disappointed Peter had decided to go back to his fishing business and for the second time we read that he worked all night without catching a thing. It is the first time we hear of him fishing in three years. I wonder if he noticed the exact same thing happening to him as three years previously? He was out all night and came back with empty nets. Jesus steps in and saves the day again.

Peter was a born leader. His decision to go fishing triggered a reaction in his companions. "We will come with you" they said. At daybreak, the time when they were probably ready to give up and get some rest, a man standing on the shore shouts to them and suggest that they were unsuccessful because the fish are on the other side of the boat. Peter does what the man suggests and casts the nets on the other side of the boat. The disciples had not recognised Jesus yet, but I think John begins to suspect, and is proved right when they cannot haul the nets in for the sheer weight of the catch! He shouts "It is the Lord"! Peter cannot hold back any longer and in his typical manner, acts before he thinks and throws himself into the sea to swim to shore, even though he was seconds away in the boat!

I think that some of the things Jesus said that day had a double meaning, dealing not only with the fishing situation, but Peter's decision to go back to his job. Jesus was talking to all the disciples, but specifically to Peter. This time Jesus is talking about casting a *single net*, not about letting down *the nets*, plural. It is more personal. When He suggests casting the net on the other side of the boat He is saying to Peter, "Why are you going back to your former life? Why did you cast your net on the wrong side of the boat? Why have you gone back to the shadow? The provision is on the other side. This time the net will not break. You can handle the catch Peter! Your future is not on that side, the fish you are supposed to be catching are on the other side. Don't you see that you are back in the shadow? Stay in the substance despite the disappointments. I have made you a fisher of men. That is what I want from you and that is what all the fish yet to be caught need from you!"

A sense of failure, guilt, shame and disappointment had driven Peter back into the shadow. He remembered his three years with the Lord, right at the beginning when he heard about Jesus preaching in the synagogues in Nazareth and Capernaum. He remembered his amazing encounter with the Master after an exhausting fruitless night, and how his mother-in-law was healed by Jesus. He remembered stepping out of the boat and walking on the water. He recalled his own words: "Even if they all fall away I will not . . . I will never disown you." But, of course he did. He did the unthinkable; he denied his Master and everybody knew it. They all remembered his arrogance when he promised he would never leave the Lord.

Yes he disowned Jesus. He ran to the empty tomb, confused, trying to overcome remorse and guilt, unable to put the different pieces of the puzzle together, unable to recall that the Master said He would rise again after three days. He could not rid his mind of the last time Jesus looked straight at him. Oh, what he would give to change the past few days! He was there when Jesus appeared to the disciples (John 20:19). I can imagine him trembling and waiting for the moment when Jesus would say, "Right Peter, let us talk about your denial and let us put it right. Let us forget about it now!" But ... nothing. Not a word! Not a single look. Peter was left with his questions, his guilt, not knowing what Jesus thought about him.

All of us will experience feelings like this one day or another. It is a lonely place to be. The heavens are closed, God is silent and the only voice you hear is the enemy telling you that you are finished. At times like this you feel that it is too hard to keep going. The only remaining option is to turn back to what you did before all this business of living in the substance and that is just what Peter did, he went fishing!

But Jesus met with him again. He had given him time to think through all this, time to back himself into the same corner he was in on the day he met Jesus for the first time! Peter denied Jesus three times, saying he did not know him and for each denial Jesus asked Peter if he loved Him. Jesus is reinstating Peter to the position he was in before the betrayal.

In fact it could be said that Peter denied the Lord four times! If we look more closely at the questions Jesus asked him: "Simon, son of John, do you love Me more than these?" Jesus calls Peter, "Son of John" or "Son of Jonas" which is quite unusual since He only called him "Son of Jonas" when He met him for the first time (John 1:42).

Jesus is reminding Peter of his background. He is underlining Peter's old identity (son of Jonas, not Cephas anymore). Peter was the son of Jonas and Jonas was a fisherman! Why is Jesus referring back to Peter's old identity? What was Peter's reaction when he heard his old name on Jesus' lips? Peter must have understood what Jesus meant, "Simon, son of a fisherman, do you love Me more than fishing, more than your work, more than the family business? If you do, follow Me and do not go back to your profession, do not go back to the shadow, but follow Me."

Peter disowned Christ four times. He pretended he did not know Him three times, but the fourth denial was when he denied Jesus' call to him to be a fisher of men and went back to his former lifestyle.

What a lesson for us all! Even when we feel ready to give up, we hear His voice from the shore of our lives inviting us to work on the right side of the boat and hang on tight to the substance of our calling so that many will benefit from His work through us. Becoming what He wants you to be is by far the most important and exciting thing in life. There is no more enjoyment anywhere; there is no greater challenge. After this incident, Peter never went back fishing. He understood once and for all that the One who said, "Follow-me", was determined to make him the best he could possibly be.

Chapter 8

Obstacles That Can Prevent Us Moving from Shadow to Substance

Character is more important than gift

We live in a society where the most gifted people are at the top, sometimes despite their poor character. In the world of sport and music, young men and women find themselves launched into a life of stardom, but were never trained to cope with the pressures that come with the package of popularity. Sex, money and power soon backfire on the majority of them. A gifted person can get the impression that everything is available to them and most of the time it is. A swarm of people serve them and some would sell their own mother to be friends with them. In the kingdom of God, things work differently, in fact the exact opposite is true. The more gifted you are, the more of a servant you must become. Jesus set the example by accepting the title of Master and therefore washing His disciples' feet (John 14:5). Leadership is about serving others and really doing it, not just talking about it! Somebody said, "We all love to talk about becoming a servant until the day we are treated like one." If you pray, "Lord, I want to serve You" then you can't complain saying, "I feel people are using me."

In visual terms, I think about gift and character as being like an iceberg. The part of the iceberg above the water is our gift. This is the part that is immediately and clearly visible to all (sometimes too visible, like those who constantly brag about their gift!). The part of the iceberg under the water is much bigger than the visible part – up to 7/10 larger, scientists have calculated – and brings stability to the whole block. The hidden part makes it "sit" in the water. This represents our character. If the character is well developed, the iceberg will be stable. If the gift is more developed than the character, the iceberg is in danger of turning upside down and exposing the smaller part (the character) while the bigger part (the gift) is submerged under the water and inoperative. Figure 2 illustrates this.

If God must make the man before He can release the ministry, He will present us with challenges so that we will be tested and show our true colours, to see if our character can sustain the anointing He desires to put upon us. The Bible is full of

Figure 2: Character and gift

examples of gifted people who were lacking in character (Samson, king Saul etc.), as well as examples of imperfect people who had character and a desire to become better (Abraham, David, Peter, to name but a few).

Moses had to spend forty years "dying" in the wilderness – dying to himself, to his selfish ambitions and hidden agendas, until the day he met his Creator who led him back to his substance, delivering the Hebrews. "What do you have in your hand?" was God's question to Moses. It is a good reminder to us that our gifts and our purpose in life must work together. The stick that Moses held in his hand symbolises "the gift". It represents the tools we will use, the things the Lord has placed in our hand so that we can do the things He has called us to do.

Moses' stick was touched by God's power and became more than a simple stick. It became a tool given by God that Moses could use, so that God could display His power through the plagues that were brought upon Egypt. Moses could not begin to wield such power until his character had been thoroughly refined. Power without character is a highly explosive combination.

Once again I must return to Peter's story as a prime example of character versus gift and observe how he was tested by the Lord before being called to fulfil his destiny. If we go back to look at his first encounter with the Lord on the shore of the sea of Galilee, following a fruitless night's fishing, we see how he is challenged and tested to the limit of his endurance by the Lord.

> *"When he had finished speaking, he said to Simon, 'Put out into the deep water and let down your nets for a catch.' Simon answered, 'Master, we've worked hard all night and haven't caught anything. But because you say so, I will let down the nets.'"*

> (Luke 5:4–5)

What a challenge Peter is facing here! After working hard all night for nothing he is desperate to go back home and rest, but an itinerant preacher borrows his boat and stands in it to teach the crowds. Peter waits for the end of the sermon so that he can go home, but Jesus challenges him to go out fishing again. Not only he is tired, disappointed and concerned about the bills he has to pay, but the biggest challenge and test of his character is staring him in the face. He has to listen to a carpenter telling him how to fish! Someone who had neither the expertise nor the qualifications required to be offering such advice.

The biggest test was for Peter to obey, even when he thought he knew better. He was the fisherman! He was the specialist, was he not? Maybe he thought, "You stick to preaching and don't interfere with my job. What if I interfered with your preaching, what would you say then?" But Peter obeyed; he went the extra mile; he did more than was naturally expected from him. He could have refused, burst out in anger and missed out completely on what Jesus wanted to show him. Then what would have happened? Would he have become the great apostle that we read about? Maybe the Lord would have given him another chance, we can only guess!

Naturally speaking it made no sense for Peter to do as Jesus said (which proves the point that obedience does not come naturally). Peter was the expert, he knew there were no fish there because he had been trying all night. I am pretty sure Jesus also knew that there were no fish. He knew Peter was right, but being the Lord, He provided them miraculously.

The point is, Peter's obedience opened a new way for him, a way that would lead him from being a fisherman to being a fisher of men, from shadow to substance. He did not allow his gift and expertise to get in the way of his obedience and trust.

We often judge situations by our ability to respond. We

become experts and we know what to do in a given situation. We measure authority by how competent people are and we find it difficult to accept an opinion when it comes from someone who is not an expert in what we do. As a musician I have often found myself in situations where I have had to agree to do something, knowing that the person asking was not the most qualified. But what seemed initially to be a ridiculous idea ended up being a great one and I had to swallow my pride. I remember when I first moved to England, Andrea and I settled in a large church where nobody knew me or my background as a musician. One evening during a musicians' practice, the worship leader was determined to show me how to play the pattern of the hi-hat for a particular song! I could have told him that he did not know who he was dealing with! I could have told him about my work in New York and everything about me, but I managed not to! Situations like these test the character.

The most gifted person is not always right, but they certainly find it difficult not to be! Character is more important than gift and if you do not allow the Lord to shape you (most of the time He does it by using others), it will be difficult for you to find your place in the wall made of living stones that we call the Church. The more gifted you are, the more work you need to do on your character, simply because you are used to your gift opening doors for you. The fact is, unless God can work on your character, many doors will remain closed for you. Because unless God is allowed to smooth all your rough edges off, you will become dangerous in ministry.

People's opinion of us

People are very good at expressing their opinions about others. We often believe we know what is best for someone else, more than we know what is best for us! Some people tend to rely heavily on what others think of them and derive much of their self-worth from the opinions of others. It is good, of course, to listen to the advice of godly people and to be accountable to one another in God's family, but if you are mostly guided by the opinions of others then it becomes a problem.

The way people see you, especially those closest to you, can influence your opinion of who you really are and this could keep you in the shadow. The fact is, your family and friends – those who have known you for the longest time – can find it difficult to see you in any other light apart from the way they have always seen you. You may have experienced this. You are still seen as the "little boy" or "little girl" who grew up in the church or in the street of your home town. Some may still call you by your childhood nick name. When you start sharing your dreams and aspirations, they cannot reconcile what they know about you and the things you talk about.

Jesus went through the same experience in His home town Nazareth. In the synagogue He opened the scroll and read and interpreted the scripture from Isaiah (Luke 4). The Bible tells us that some of the people were amazed, but others were offended. This is not a contradiction; for some the sight of "little Jesus" all grown up and standing in front of the whole town reading the scroll, would have been enough for them to marvel, just like a grandma listening to her grandchildren playing the piano on her birthday. But for the elders, the religious Jews, those who understood the scriptures, it was different.

"Isn't this the carpenter's son? Isn't his mother's name Mary, and aren't his brothers James, Joseph, Simon and Judas? Aren't all his sisters with us? Where then did this man learn all these things?" they said and they took offence. They had a problem with the fact He was claiming to be the fulfilment of what

He read about, but also, they couldn't see beyond the little boy, the carpenter's son, who was probably considered "Mary's illegitimate boy".

Jesus concluded that a prophet is without honour in his home town and in his own house. The Bible tells us that not a great deal could be done there in Nazareth because of the people's incredulity. The people failed to see Jesus the Saviour, the Christ, announced in the Scriptures. They failed to see Jesus in His substance, His destiny. In their understanding they had defined Him as the "grown up carpenter". They could not see further.

When my desire to preach the Word of God began to grow, it was so difficult to convince some of my family and friends. They just couldn't see it. I was Gaby the musician and they could not imagine me as a preacher. This was worsened by the fact that at that time in France, a preacher preached and a musician played in the worship band and the two did not mix – what a tragedy! When the Lord called me out of France, He put me in a place where people did not know me as a musician. There I could make a start, safely and without having to face the doubts of those around me who thought they knew me best, when in fact they only knew one aspect of me.

Some of my old friends who saw me in France after a gap of three or four years, told me how much I had changed and I would partially agree! My character had changed, but essentially I had simply moved on from the shadow into the substance. The most important thing is that the substance had always been in me! I thank God for the few faithful people who saw it and helped me to achieve it. We need more people who are able to see potential in others. Jesus saw Peter as a fisherman who would become a fisher of men. The Lord trusted in the seed that was planted in him, ready to grow at the sound of deep calling to deep.

Fear of leaving familiar shores

The French writer André Gide[3] said,

> "One doesn't discover new lands without consenting to lose sight of the shore for a very long time"

In the same way that Jesus asked Peter to pull out into deep waters and even later to step out of the boat, the Lord will most certainly challenge us at some stage in life to a greater step of faith than we have ever taken before.

I remember the time when my wife and I felt it was time to move on from where we were, but hesitated with the fear of the unknown, fear of losing what we were sure of. I was one of the staff in a great church where I was learning a great deal about leadership and my wife had a full-time job as a school teacher. After five years we began to feel increasingly unsettled in our spirit. Our desire was to serve the French speaking nations and it was difficult to do it with two full-time jobs in England.

My position was, "Lord, you have established me here for the past five years, tell me what I should do. I feel unsettled. Am I still where I should be?"

That day I went home and looked at my clockwork metronome and I thought back to the time when I was teaching percussion. The metronome can be a percussionist's best friend or worst enemy because it tells him whether he is in time or not! I remember saying to my students, "You know when you are perfectly in time because you can no longer hear the metronome." If you play exactly on the beat of the metronome you can't hear it. If you can, it means that you are not perfectly in time and need to readjust your tempo.

As I remembered this I realised that the Lord was speaking to me! When you are where you are supposed to be, doing what you are supposed to do, you do not need the Spirit of God to tell you on every single beat that you are in time, doing the right thing, do you? You do not need constantly to *hear* a confirmation from the Lord when you are walking at His pace, because you are already on the "beat" of His Spirit.

If the tempo of the metronome speeds up or slows down while you are still playing, you will certainly feel out of sync and clearly hear the beat of the metronome at odds with you. Similarly, if the Lord changes pace and you make no adjustment, you will equally feel out of sync with Him and unsettled.

My wife and I were feeling unsettled and out of sync simply because the Lord had changed tempo and we were not on His beat anymore. I believe that there are many who realise that they are no longer in sync with the Lord, but they will not make a move for fear of the unknown, the fear of leaving the comfort and security they have to move into an undefined future. After a while, they get used to living out of sync and even blame the devil for their struggle as the ultimate excuse. Their life is focused on the past and not on the future.

A few weeks later, during a Christmas vacation in France, another situation opened my eyes and ears so that the voice of the Lord was heard with great clarity. I was walking in the city centre looking for a mini-bank. The cash point was inside the foyer of the bank and to get it, I had to go through two doors. For security reasons, the two doors cannot be opened together. You had to use your credit card to open the first door and only when that door was firmly closed behind you, could you open the second door leading to the cash machine.

Not realising this, I went through the first door and tried to open the second one in front of me before the door behind me was closed. Of course, it wouldn't open and a little indicator light on the door remained red until I closed the door behind me. Only then, a green light appeared and I was able to get through to the cash point. I heard the Lord clearly telling me, "You cannot open the door of the future unless you close the door of the past." I stayed there in the mini bank for ages pondering what I had just heard. I realised that I needed to look forward and forget the past. I needed to close the door of the past, thank God for all the good people I had met and for all the valuable experience I had gained and open the door of the future to the unknown, the door of faith!

I realised I was trying to keep both doors open at once. I wanted to keep all my options open. I wanted the future, yes, but with the past tagging along too, just in case. I wanted to follow the Lord (the door of the future), but with all the security I depended on (the door of the past). I knew then that we would not step into God's plans for us until we were prepared to make the first move by closing the door on what we were currently doing.

My wife Andy, only a short while after this experience of mine, woke up one morning with this thought in her mind, "Stop your natural provision, then I will send the ravens." This refers to 1 Kings 17, when Elijah was told that he should go and hide in the Kerith Ravine. He would drink from the brook and the Lord would command ravens to feed him. We clearly understood that Andy too had to give up her teaching job and *then* we would see the provision of the Lord.

We spoke to our leaders and they released us with their blessing since we all felt the Lord was in it. We found ourselves without jobs and without a salary, but with the conviction that we had done the right thing. However, the day came when our conviction was put to the test. We were in France, walking on a mountain path leading to a cliff with a beautiful view over the valley below when we both felt that maybe we had made a mistake in leaving everything behind.

Doubt came and enveloped us until we were unable to think clearly about what we had done. Maybe we should have waited a little longer to leave our jobs? As the words were still on our lips, two big black crows flew out of a bush and circled above our heads for a long time calling out, "Kwah, kwah, kwah."

In French the word *crois*, roughly pronounced "kwah", means "BELIEVE"! The "ravens" of God's provision were bawling at us, "Believe, believe, believe!" The Lord would provide and we knew it for sure then. We knew not in our heads, but deep in our hearts. We knew that even if the spiritual "brook" were to dry up, it would only be because the Lord had something else for us and it is His way of moving us on. A dried up brook may look like a closed door to some, but for those who love and trust the Lord it is the assurance that another door is about to open. He promised that He will never leave us nor forsake us. Today when we look back we can testify that He has always been faithful!

The love of lifestyle and the comfort of money can stop us from getting into the substance of the Lord's promise for us. We live in a very uncertain world where a good family, a good job and a nice house can lure us to believe that we have achieved our ultimate goal. These things are important and good but they are not the primary purpose of our lives. The day we stand before Christ He will not judge us primarily on these things, but on how well we have run the race marked out for us!

The enemy of our soul knows this only too well and he will try every trick in the book to keep us busy with the mundane affairs of life. It is interesting to observe the strategy that Pharaoh used when he was dealing with the Israelites during their time of slavery in Egypt when Moses was giving them the hope of a better life in the Promised Land:

> *"Afterwards Moses and Aaron went to Pharaoh and said, 'This is what the* LORD, *the God of Israel, says: "Let my people go, so that they may hold a festival to me in the desert."'*
>
> *Pharaoh said, 'Who is the* LORD, *that I should obey him and let Israel go? I do not know the* LORD *and I will not let Israel go.'*
>
> *Then they said, 'The God of the Hebrews has met with us. Now let us take a three-day journey into the desert to offer sacrifices to the* LORD *our God, or he may strike us with plagues or with the sword.'*
>
> *But the king of Egypt said, 'Moses and Aaron, why are you taking the people away from their labour? Get back to your work!' Then Pharaoh said, 'Look, the people of the land are now numerous, and you are stopping them from working.'*
>
> *That same day Pharaoh gave this order to the slave drivers and foremen in charge of the people: 'You are no longer to supply the people with straw for making bricks; let them go and gather their own straw. But require them to make the same number of bricks as before; don't reduce the quota. They are lazy; that is why they are crying out, "Let us go and sacrifice to our God." Make the work harder for the men so that they keep working and pay no attention to lies.'*
>
> *Then the slave drivers and the foremen went out and said to the people, 'This is what Pharaoh says: "I will not give you any more straw. Go and get your own straw wherever you can find it, but your work will not be reduced at all."' So the people scattered all over Egypt to gather stubble to use for straw. The slave drivers kept pressing them, saying, 'Complete the work required of you for each day, just as when you had straw.' The Israelite foremen appointed by Pharaoh's slave drivers were*

*beaten and were asked, 'Why didn't you meet your quota of
bricks yesterday or today, as before?'*

*Then the Israelite foremen went and appealed to Pharaoh:
'Why have you treated your servants this way? Your servants are
given no straw, yet we are told, "Make bricks!" Your servants are
being beaten, but the fault is with your own people.'*

*Pharaoh said, 'Lazy, that's what you are – lazy! That is why
you keep saying, "Let us go and sacrifice to the LORD."' "*

(Exodus 5:1–17)

Sent by the Lord, Moses went to Pharaoh and asked him to let
the Israelites go so that they could offer a sacrifice to God. The
Lord was calling His people out of slavery and into a life of
destiny and purpose. Pharaoh knew that this would be an
unhelpful distraction for the Israelites and it would certainly
affect their work, so he took appropriate measures.

The first thing he did was to give orders to the foremen not to
supply the people with any more straw for making bricks, even
though the same number of bricks had to be produced. In other
words, Pharaoh was making the work much harder for the
Israelites.

For a long time I read this story as another example of the
cruelty of Pharaoh and the pain endured by the people of God. I
understood that the lesson to learn from it was, we who were
once in the grip of Satan (the Pharaoh of this age), were kept in
captivity until our "Moses" (Jesus), came to deliver us from
slavery, from our sins that were keeping us shackled. But there is
another very important lesson in all this.

The reason Pharaoh made the Israelite's work harder was not
simply to increase their suffering, but to *distract them* so that they
could not listen to Moses! Notice verse 9 says, *"Make the work
harder for the men so that they keep working **and pay no attention to**

lies" (emphasis added). The people became so consumed by trying to find out how to get their own straw that they had no time to listen to Moses, a man sent by God to lead them into the Promised Land!

For us, the people of God who live in "Egypt" (the world in which we live), the danger is to become so busy with our work and the pursuit of gathering "straw" to pay our mortgages and buy our cars, that we fail to hear the voice of the Lord and play into the hands of the devil by living a meaningless life of superficial Christianity.

The second thing Pharaoh did was to sow a very powerful thought in the people's mind, a thought that said that sacrifice, or worship, is for those who are lazy and have nothing to do; it is for those who want to avoid hard work. Those who work hard have no time for going off into the desert to worship. Pharaoh was trying to make them feel guilty for wanting to spend time before the Lord. A very powerful weapon indeed which is still in operation today, you may be interested to know! How many people think in negative terms about setting aside long periods of time to pray or worship; to take a few days off to seek the Lord? "I can't afford that sort of time," they say. "I've got work to do and a house to run." The idea that working hard is an indication of a healthy spiritual life is as absurd as the idea that we should spend *all* our time lost in praise and wonder.

The answer is in finding balance, but the point I am making here is how easy it is to be trapped by a lie. Pharaoh knew it and he used it, so does our enemy!

Negotiating with the Lord

Another obstacle that can prevent us from moving from shadow to substance is the trap of trying to negotiate with God. In the story of Luke 5 that we read previously, notice that Peter didn't try to draw Jesus into his fishing business! Think about it. Peter could have seen Jesus as the hen that lays golden eggs. With Jesus' help Peter could have made a fortune! But Peter was invited to follow Jesus and whether he understood what the Lord meant by "From now on, you will catch men" or not, he still left everything and obeyed without trying to negotiate with Jesus.

We are often ready to do God's work, but on our terms. We pretend that we are following the Lord, when in fact we are trying to get Him to follow us and our agenda. This will never get us anywhere. If anything, it will only cause delay. We follow Jesus because He is going somewhere and wants us to follow after Him. When we do, we are changed during the journey. He will make me the very best of us, but on His terms not ours.

When the Lord called to Moses from the burning bush (Exodus 3), He asked him to take off his sandals (verse 5). Much has been written about the fact that Moses was barefoot in the presence of God: the fact that God's holiness cannot be taken lightly, that nothing impure or dirty like the sole of a sandal covered in the dust of the desert can enter holy ground. I am sure all this is true, but there is another thought that I would like to share with you.

In the story of Ruth (Ruth 4), Boaz wanted to marry her and he went up to the town gate where he sat waiting for the kinsman-redeemer to see if he wanted to buy the land belonging to their brother Elimelech. Verse 7 goes on to say that previously in Israel, in order for the redemption and transfer of property to become final, one party took off his sandal and gave it to the other. This was the method of finalising transactions in Israel. The giving of the sandal was equivalent to the signature on a contract today. What would a man do then if he had no sandals? He would not be able to buy anything! Slaves had bare feet and had no rights whatsoever. They were unable to negotiate at all! Moses, barefoot without his sandals was put in a no-negotiation situation. He was symbolically unable to bargain or negotiate with the call from the Lord to set the Israelites free and became a "slave" of the Lord. Moses however, attempted to negotiate and propose a different deal – *"Oh Lord, please send someone else to do it"* (Exodus 4:13) – and the Lord became angry.

When Joshua, Moses' disciple, was about to enter Jericho (Joshua 5:13), he looked up and saw a man standing before him with a drawn sword in his hand. He asked him, *"Are you for us or for our enemies?"* He got an unusual response: *"Neither"* (verse 14). Joshua fell face down on the ground in reverence and asked him, *"What message does my Lord have for his servant?"* (verse 14). The commander of the army of the Lord replied. *"Take off your sandals for the place where you are standing is holy."*

Here again there were no negotiations. The "neither" might have simply meant, "Wrong question! This has nothing to do with whether I am with you or not. But it has everything to do with you being with me! I am leading you into Jericho. You follow me." Joshua probably recognised the status of this commander (the Lord Himself) which explains why he fell face down to the ground in reverence and did not try to negotiate with Him.

Not thirsty enough

Another obvious stumbling block on the road to moving forward into the substance of the will of God is a lack of appetite for the things of the kingdom of God. If you are not hungry and thirsty enough for God, you will find it difficult to leave your comfort zone. Rather you will be satisfied with a non-committal type of Christianity. Those satisfied with the world, who see no need of Christ, do not thirst. But by His grace, God can give us a thirst and desire for Him, a thirst that only He can quench.

Isaiah 55:1 says this,

> *"Come, all you who are thirsty,*
> *come to the waters;*
> *and you who have no money,*
> *come, buy and eat!*
> *Come, buy wine and milk*
> *without money and without cost."*

Come and buy even without money? That's what the Bible says doesn't it? How can we buy without money? It is possible when the currency is not money, but a thirst and a hunger for God. Thirst and hunger for God will buy us an entry ticket to all the riches He has for us. They are not free! The Bible clearly states that you must buy them with your desire for the Lord. They are accessible to those who seek Him *earnestly*. If we are not thirsty enough or hungry enough we cannot receive them.

The Bible says in Psalm 25:14

> *"The secret of the* LORD *is for those who fear Him,*
> *And He will make them know His covenant."*

(NASB)

Today, too many Christians have lost their thirst and hunger for God, especially in Europe. They come to their Sunday morning meetings and drift along through the worship time and the preaching of the Word. We have understood the importance of allowing our children to stay during the worship, but then have allowed them to bring along their own entertainment to keep them quietly occupied and their parents happy!

In some ways we are responsible for the loss of hunger for God in people. We have allowed our meetings to become a place of entertainment, but because we will never match (and should not even try) what the world has to offer in terms of entertainment, the people get bored. They listen to the same songs over and over, the band is too loud, the congregation cannot hear itself and the worship leader (should I call him the song leader?) gets frustrated by the lack of response.

The result is that the people sit down and become spectators of what is often just a poor performance. Some have understood this and have begun to work on the quality of the performance. They provide huge, well-equipped stages with sound and lights and a great team of skilled musicians. Do not misunderstand me, I think it is important that we give the Lord the best we can. Excellence has always been part of the equation as far as worship is concerned in the Bible and after so many years of drought and mediocrity I am encouraged to see people using their gifts to honour God and it should carry on. But we must be aware of the danger of confusing encountering God and entertainment. Let us not try to put the Ark of God on a Philistine cart again! Let us be determined not to bring the "world" into the Church, but rather take the Church into the world.

I agree with those who say that in order to do that, we need to present excellence to those who do not know Christ. But the line is not always drawn clearly enough and the people of God are beginning to be very choosy. They know what they want and how they want it. It is very much like during the time of Eli the priest when the servant of the priest would come with a three-pronged fork in his hand while the meat was being boiled, whenever anyone offered a sacrifice (1 Samuel 2:13). The servant of the priest would say, *"Give the priest some meat to roast; he won't accept boiled meat from you, but only raw"* (1 Samuel 2:15).

The fat had to be offered to God before the servant could take any meat for the priest, but the priest demanded raw meat. Why was that? I think he wanted raw meat so that he could cook it the way he liked it, rare, medium or well done!

Some Christians today choose the type of meeting they want. Some want the worship very well cooked while others prefer it raw! They prefer a certain kind of music or another. They come with their three-pronged fork in order to take everything they can. We have almost encouraged this attitude in them by providing entertainment instead of reverence, producing in people a desire to take instead of giving. Christian life is all about giving! Worship is more than a list of songs! More than music! These are only expressions of it. Worship is about giving to God, it is responding to His presence whether we feel like it or not. If we compromise this principle we allow apathy and entertainment to pave the way and one day we will pay the price for it, probably with the next generation.

There is an interesting story in the Bible that illustrates this imbalance and how it affected the people of God for several generations. In 1 Samuel 6:13 when the Philistines got rid of the Ark, it arrived at Beth Shemesh and it is surprising to see the lack of respect shown by the inhabitants of Beth Shemesh for the Ark of God. They put it on a large rock with the chest containing the gold objects and worshipped the Ark *and* the golden "idols" next to it! Then, if that was not enough, they decided to look inside the Ark, bringing judgment and death upon themselves.

These people were actually Israelites They were the people of God. There were Levites among them – the priestly line! Should they not have known? Where and when did it go all wrong? The answer is found in Judges 1:33 at the end of the battle for the Promised Land.

The Lord had very clearly warned the Israelites not to make any covenant with the people of the land, but to break down their altars. The tribe of Naphtali did not obey. They did not drive out the inhabitants Beth Shemesh. What a surprise! The same Beth Shemesh that was mentioned in 1 Samuel. They were rebuked by the angel of the Lord (Judges 2) and wept a lot, but did not fix the problem. As a result, the problem (the inhabitants and their heathen worship) became a stumbling block for the following generations as well. They compromised God's principle and ended-up tolerating all the pagan worship around them until it became part of their lives. They conformed to the pattern, the fashion of their time and it is hardly surprising that many years later when the Ark appeared in the fields of Beth Shemesh, their children didn't think twice about sitting it alongside the Philistines' idols or looking into it without fear or respect for the presence of God. "Who can stand in the presence of the Lord this holy God?" they asked, but it was the wrong question. Not "who can stand" but "how should we stand" in the presence of God.

If we don't teach the next generation how to stand in His presence, how we need to thirst and hunger for God; If we do not impart the fact that we do not come in the presence of our Lord and King to be entertained, but to bring Him our praise, our lives, our joys and our sorrows, we will pay a very expensive price in the near future. In other words, if we do not bring the Ark of the covenant back into our gatherings, our churches and our homes, the apathy we see today will be but a shadow of what we should expect to see tomorrow. We will not enter into the substance of what God has for us as a nation or as individuals.

Paul says it very clearly in Romans 12. He talks about the highest kind of sacrifice. He calls it *"your spiritual act of worship"* (Romans 12:1), which is the offering of our bodies as living sacrifices. It is more than a song, more than a Sunday morning service, it is a lifestyle of giving thanks to God at work, at school, at home – a life that thirsts after Him, a life that can never have enough of His presence.

Don't you find it strange that in 1 Samuel 7 when the Ark was left for twenty years in the house of a man called Abinadab, the Bible doesn't mention Abinadab's family until, at the end of the twenty years, his son Uzzah is killed by the Lord for having touched the Ark? They had gotten used to having the Ark in their home. They had become so familiar with the presence of God that Uzzah thought he could walk in front of the Ark and even touch it. By contrast, in 2 Samuel 6:10 the Ark was left for three months in the house of Obed-Edom. The Bible goes on to say that the Lord blessed his household and everything he had to the point that even King David heard about it.

The difference between these two homes was the attitude and the thirst and hunger for God. In fact Obed-Edom so loved the presence of God that later on, when David took the Ark to Jerusalem, he became a door keeper in the house of the Lord!

When I was in infant school, Bruno, my class-mate told me he had a secret he wanted to show me. Obviously I had to assure him that I would not breathe a word to anyone. His secret became our secret, and no one else could ever know about it. After school that day he took me to the field behind his house. There, under a stone he had hidden a bag filled with beautiful multicoloured marbles. Bruno saw my face light up when I laid eyes on his treasure and he started laughing. His whole body shook and he doubled up in fits of laughter. My unreserved admiration gave him such joy!

From then on I was thrilled to be able to sneak into that field any time I wanted and take out those marbles of every colour and size you could imagine. We used to sit for hours studying them, holding them up to the sun so that their colours would shine even more. So that he could hold on to the joy of the moment and keep on reliving the experience, Bruno used to add other marbles from time to time to surprise me and each time it was like the first time over again, my explosion of joy and Bruno rolling on the floor with laughter!

The problem with Bruno was that he could not keep the secret to himself. It was too much to ask. Too much joy, excitement and laughter to keep it just between the two of us. I quickly understood that the real "buzz" for him was in the telling of his secret and seeing the reaction of the chosen few. The news quickly spread, but not everyone came to the field. It just did not interest some of our class-mates. Others were content with their own collections and some had so many marbles nothing could impress them. For me, however, those little gems were the most beautiful thing in the world, partly because they were pretty, but most importantly because they were *hidden*. You had to want to see them and go to find them. The quest and the effort involved gave me pleasure upon pleasure.

This little story illustrates very well our attitude towards God. He wants to surprise us. He wants us to marvel at all the riches He has for us. He cannot help but reveal Himself and kiss those who thirst and hunger for Him.

One winter's night in 1992, I went up into the mountains near Grenoble in France, where I lived. I went to pray as I did several times each week. I had my favourite place, a hillside that sat above a forest and looked over the mountainside. It was very cold, a particular kind of cold you feel in the Alps at that time of year. The sky was totally clear and from it shone thousands and thousands of stars. As it was late, the surrounding area was silent and the quiet was only broken from time to time by the far off cry of a fox or an owl. I started to worship the Lord and thank Him for His magnificent creation and the beauty that surrounded me. The desire to worship and adore Him flowed over me like waves and I stayed in His presence for ages.

Then all of a sudden I heard the sound of a breeze. A very gentle breeze blew in over the tops of the trees a few hundred metres in front of me. The breeze caught my attention because it broke the silence of the night and its sound gradually became louder, like a crescendo. The nearer it came to me, passing through the forest, the more I felt the presence of God. I closed my eyes and opened my arms wide as if to embrace His presence. A warm wind enveloped me and touched my face. Then, I smelt a sweet perfume, an extraordinary perfume. This experience lasted just a moment, but I wanted time to stand still. Then, back to the silence, not a single sound.

I know that the Lord met with me in a unique way. This experience convinced me that in the secret place, God's presence is tangible. He invites us, He waits for us, He wants us to search for Him and to desire His presence. He wants us to be thirsty for Him!

Have I wasted my life? Is it too late?

I have had a few concerned people react to the teaching about shadow and substance by telling me, "That is fine when you are young and still have the choice, but what do you do when you have wasted your years? Can I still be useful and reach the substance of my real potential? Is it too late?"

My conviction is NO! It is never too late with the Lord, there is always hope.

The Bible says in Joel 2:25,

> *"I will repay you for the years the locusts have eaten –*
>   *the great locust and the young locust,*
>   *the other locusts and the locust swarm –*
> *my great army that I sent among you."*

The Lord is able to give us back some of the fruit of those wasted years when we recognise our responsibility and repent of our negligence.

In the context of Joel, the Lord was the one who sent the locusts! So how much more will He do for us regarding the things that He did not take from us, but that we wasted through our own negligence? I think it is fair to say that He will repay us for some of the years and not all of them! Sin is pardonable, but some of its consequences will last until we die. Our actions have a consequence and some of them will continue even after we have been forgiven. A criminal can repent and receive God's forgiveness, but he will still have to pay the penalty of time in prison. For those who are in prison for their faith in Jesus, their repayment may happen in heaven. For all who are in Christ, the full repayment of what Satan has stolen in the Garden of Eden will be given in heaven: eternity with the Father!

Much can be redeemed during our time on earth. We talked earlier about the gifts that have been given to us which provide a clear indication of our destiny in Christ. In the context of trying to deal with wasted years, let us not forget that we will not use all the gifts we have for our whole life. Experience is the greatest gift of all and one we will never wear out. It is a tragedy when older people say, "I've had my time. There's nothing left for me to do now." We desperately need the wisdom and experience of the former generation. Surely we can learn from their mistakes as well as their successes. Let us give them room so that their ultimate gift, the experience of their lifetime will not be buried and wasted forever!

In this chapter we have looked at a number of obstacles that will hinder us from moving from the shadow into the substance. In the final chapter we will look at a single obstacle, perhaps the most prevalent of all, that is a barrier for many: the temptation to want to be someone else.

Note

1. French critic, essayist and novelist (1869–1951).

Chapter 9

The Temptation to Want to Be Someone Else

Such is the world that we live in that one can easily feel under tremendous pressure to conform to the pattern of this age, which tells us that those who are successful must, by definition, be good looking, slim, talented and rich. Many young people today have no ambition other than to become famous, because fame, they think, will bring them all these other assets. The media has perpetuated this myth by generating all kinds of reality shows and music programmes where image is more important than true gift and certainly more important than character. It tells the young people watching that if they want success and fame they should follow the role models they see on TV or read about in magazines.

Music, sport and cinema convey powerful images of success and they have become the blank canvas, the pattern, the mindset so many want to follow. Many professions are being lost because of it. Who wants to be a farmer, a baker or a carpenter these days? Sadly some jobs are viewed as "substandard" by the young generation who will not be satisfied with anything less than a "high profile" career. This is okay for some, but for others it could result in them missing out on God's plan for their lives.

Many are attracted by the stage and the pulpit, and seek the thrill of having authority over people. They want to be "like" a famous preacher they have seen. They soon find out however, that they are not in the right place in the kingdom of God and excitement gives way to disappointment and bitterness. We should always aim to be the best we can be, but this can only be achieved through Christ. He is the only One who can bring the best out of you, whether your destiny is to become a pop star, a tennis player, a musician, a farmer, a preacher or a bank manager. God knows what He has in store for you and demands that you resist the temptation of trying to be what you are not meant to be.

The Bible has a few things to say on the subject of the man who gives in to the desire to be somebody else. If you believe that the Lord knew you before you were born and that He prepared good works in advance for you to do on the earth, then you must also believe that you need to be the "real you" in order to move into the substance of your calling. The Word of God underlines the fact that if you lose your identity, you lose your inheritance.

The story of Jacob is a striking example of a man who was uncomfortable with who he was. Jacob tried to change his identity on three occasions, revealing the fact that he actually wanted to be his brother, Esau! The story begins in Genesis 25:21 where the Bible tells us that twenty years after Isaac got married, the Lord answered his prayer for his barren wife. She became pregnant and since she couldn't go for a scan as we would do today, she enquired of the Lord. The verdict was unmistakable, two babies. Two "nations" were in her womb and the Lord said that the older would serve the younger! This was unusual since the firstborn generally inherited a double portion and would be served by the younger child. But, the Lord knew what would happen many years later.

When the time came for Rebekah to give birth, the first child was born and his body was like a hairy garment. He was named Esau. Then his brother was born, with his hand *grasping* Esau's heel! It was as if the second baby was striving to be born first. For that reason they named him Jacob, meaning "the one who deceives". Little did he know that ultimately he deceived himself just as much as he deceived others.

This is the first of three examples of Jacob wanting to be Esau, the firstborn. What were his reasons? He probably wanted to inherit the double portion due to the firstborn son. Years later, when the babies have grown into young men, the Bible tells us what kind of men they were (Genesis 25:27). Esau had become a skilful hunter, a man of the open country, whereas Jacob was more the meditative type, staying at home among the tents. Perhaps, because of this, he became a good cook, learning from his mother Rebekah? The smell of stew was so tempting for Esau coming back from the woods ravenous after a day's hunting. Jacob made a deal with his brother: a portion of stew in exchange for his birthright! Here is Jacob's second attempt to steal Esau's identity. The birthright belongs to the firstborn. Esau was the firstborn regardless of Jacob's attempt to come first. By stealing the birthright, Jacob symbolically changes his identity and "becomes" Esau.

The third, successful attempt, was when his father Isaac was very old. Jacob took advantage of Isaac's age. His eyes were so weak that he could no longer see (Genesis 27). Sensing that his days were coming to an end, Isaac prepared to bless his children. He told Esau to go hunting and then prepare his favourite food.

Jacob found an accomplice in his mother Rebekah and they proceeded to trick Isaac by preparing the meal he had asked Esau to make for him. Jacob received the blessing of the firstborn that was rightfully Esau's. He put on Esau's clothes so that he smelled like him and covered his hands and the smooth parts of his neck with goats skin so that if Isaac touched him, he would think he was touching Esau. As for the two young goats required, he did not have to hunt for them since he took them from their flock.

Jacob approached his father (disguised as Esau) and spoke to him. Isaac, unable to see, had to rely on his ears. He was a bit confused! He said, "Who is it?" and then later, "Come near so that I can touch you my son to know whether you really are my son Esau or not." Isaac was clearly not sure. When he finally touched his son, he said something very interesting: *"The voice is the voice of Jacob, but the hands are the hands of Esau"* (Genesis 27:22)! The fact is that Jacob chose to trust what he touched more than what he heard! In a world that is seeking emotional experiences and is increasingly interested in following feelings, we should remember the dimension of faith which comes from *hearing* the Lord and not from feeling or touching!

Jacob stole Esau's blessing from his father and nothing could change it, not even Esau's loud and bitter cry or copious tears. This was the third time that Jacob had tried to steal Esau's identity and it looked as though this time he had done it.

In all this it seems that the Lord remained silent, but we will see what lesson he taught Jacob. I said earlier that changing your identity means changing your inheritance. This is what the Lord is about to teach Jacob.

Jacob paid a great price for his deceptions. Firstly, he was forced to leave home for around twenty years. He went to the north west of Mesopotamia to a place called Paddan Arran where he stayed in the house of his grandfather Bethuel. He was instructed by Isaac to marry one of his uncle Laban's daughters.

Laban had two daughters, Leah and Rachel. Jacob fell in love with Rachel. In fact he was so in love with her that he agreed to work for seven years for her hand in marriage. After the completion of the seven years the time had come for the marriage to be celebrated and here we see the Lord's response to Jacob's identity crisis! First, we need a bit of a cultural background to help us understand what the Bible is saying.

At that time certain rules had to be strictly observed as far as marriages were concerned:

- Our forefathers practised *endogamy* – the practice or rule of marrying only within one's own family group. This is precisely why Isaac instructed Jacob to take a wife from among the daughters of Laban, Rebekah's brother (Genesis 28:2). This is also why Abraham made his servant swear that he would not get a wife for his son Isaac from the daughters of the Canaanites, but from his own relatives (Genesis 24:3–4)

- The eldest child of one family had to marry the eldest child of the other family and the youngest child of one family had to marry the youngest child of the other family. The eldest child had to marry first. This explains Laban's answer to a mesmerised and angry Jacob who found out that he had been tricked by him, giving him Leah instead of Rachel after serving his seven years: *"It is not our custom here to give the younger daughter in marriage before the older one"* (Genesis 29:26).

- The bride was always veiled. Her head and face were covered. We will see why this is very important in the context of Jacob's wedding.

- A maidservant was given to the bride-to-be as soon as the wedding was announced. Genesis 29:24 at first seems to contradict this, but it doesn't. It simply explains how Laban managed to trick Jacob.

Jacob loved Rachel and was about to marry her. The youngest child of one family had to marry the youngest of the other family, which was perfect for Jacob since he was the youngest son and was in love with Rachel, Laban's youngest daughter.

Here is the lesson I believe the Lord taught Jacob. Jacob had proved three times that he wanted to "be" Esau and in a sense he did "become" Esau. But consequently he inherited Esau's portion, which was Leah! Leah was the eldest child like Esau, so she should have been Esau's inheritance. By becoming Esau, Jacob got Esau's inheritance. By changing his identity, Jacob changed his inheritance. (See figure 3.)

After the wedding ceremony, I wonder what Jacob's reaction was when he realised he was in bed with Leah and not Rachel? In the same way seven years earlier his father Isaac asked him, "Is that you Esau?" the deceiver had been deceived. It was pay back time for Jacob who so desperately wanted to escape his true identity.

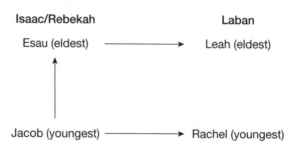

Figure 3: Jacob's inheritance in marriage

Here is a striking lesson for all of us. If we change our identity we change our inheritance in the Lord. It is difficult to go from the shadow to the substance if we are not ourselves; if we spend our lives trying to be what we are not called to be, carrying a burden that is not ours. It is interesting to note that one of the roots of the name Leah is "weary". How many believers, ministers, churches are carrying a "Leah" instead of a "Rachel"? How many have changed their identity as people or churches or mission organisations? They have substituted Leah for Rachel. They have given in to the pressure to conform to the latest trend, the latest fashion in ministry, but after a while they feel and look tired, heavy laden and disillusioned. They had a beautiful Rachel, a God-given vision, but they are carrying a Leah, a manmade ministry and they are weary!

Another question remains and in answering it there is a lot more that we can learn from Jacob's painful experience. How on earth was Laban able to trick Jacob? It is not a common occurrence to marry the wrong lady. It is not usual to wake up after your honeymoon night with the wrong bride! But Jacob's bride was veiled and throughout the wedding ceremony he would not have been able to see her face. The cunning of Laban proved too much for a Jacob blinded by love.

The custom at the time required that a maidservant be given to the bride as soon as the wedding was announced. So, as soon as Jacob declared his love for Rachel and spoke to Laban, a maidservant was appointed to her. For seven years Rachel's maidservant helped her to prepare for her wedding. She would have been known as Rachel's maidservant. On the wedding day she would have acted in the capacity of bridesmaid. The name of Rachel's maidservant was Zilpah.

Laban managed to substitute Leah for Rachel by presenting a heavily veiled (unidentifiable) Leah, with Rachel's maidservant

Zilpah attending her! Jacob could not see his bride's veiled face, but he could clearly identify her maidservant Zilpah, the one who had helped Rachel prepare for this particular day for seven years! It was enough to convince him! The right servant serving the wrong bride.

It is my conviction that when the Lord gives us a vision, a job to do, He also provides the right fellow workers; those who share your passion for the job. Because of the shared passion there is a great chance that they will have the right qualifications for the task. These will be good servants, people who will put in the hours without counting and will be loyal and faithful. If you change the vision however, all these servants will find themselves serving the wrong vision. They will be like Zilpah, the right servant but serving the wrong master or vision. Changing the identity of the vision (unless clearly instructed by the Spirit of God) is a guarantee that many of the people sent by the Lord to help to work at the task will find them- selves confused and out of sync with God's mandate. They will be forced to leave, or worse, they will conform to serving a Leah when they were called to serve a Rachel. Some types of ministries attract more people than others and for the sake of being popular many change direction, leaving those who came to serve the primary vision in total confusion. The shadow and the substance have a lot in common. The shadow is the silhouette of the substance. To change identity is like changing the shadow. The shadow will not match the substance any more and that is impossible.

Jacob had to work for seven more years to marry Rachel. After a total of twenty years the Lord called him back to his homeland. In a way, Jacob's future was in his past, a past that he now had to face, a past called Esau! The ford of Jabbok (meaning "emptying") that he crossed in Genesis 32:22 was symbolic of an empty Jacob trying to find the willpower to go back to what would probably be the worst event of his life.

At Jabbok, Jacob was forced to wrestle with an angel of the Lord. His wrestling with the angel was also symbolic of Jacob wrestling with himself. He was fearful because he had heard that Esau was coming to meet him with four hundred men! So after wrestling all night, he demanded a blessing. He didn't steal this one this time, but fought all night for it. What blessing was Jacob asking for? Deliverance from his brother? If so, then he got the worse possible result, facing four hundred men with his hip out of place! No, I think there is something more in his demand. The angel of the Lord knew very well what kind of blessing Jacob needed. He asked, *"What is your name?"* (Genesis 32:27). The angel was putting his finger directly on Jacob's problem: his name, his identity! Jacob had fought so hard all his life to be somebody else. The angel restored Jacob's identity and he changed his name to "Israel". That was the blessing, being what he was ordained to be from before creation. No longer the deceiver, but a man through whom God's plan for humanity would prevail.

A few thousand years later, little David, called to be Saul's successor, faced Goliath. After trying on Saul's armour on he said, *"I cannot go in these ... because I am not used to them"* (1 Samuel 17:39). Thank God that David did not persist in trying to get used to something that was simply not his. He could have wanted to look like the king and what better way than to wear his armour! But no, he preferred to face one of the biggest challenges of his life as himself, a shepherd boy with his staff, his pouch, five smooth stones and a sling in his hand.

Jesus wants you to be yourself so that He can take you into deeper waters in Him. There is a real danger in trying to be someone else, the risk of missing God's best!

Conclusion

God wants to bring all things from the shadow into the substance.
He is building His Church. We need to see the bigger picture of
what Christianity is all about. Too many believers are occupying a
chair in a church once or twice a week with little idea of what
they could be in Christ. Too many unbelievers need to see Jesus
as the only One who can make them the best they could ever be,
but they need to see it in us first. In my travelling I come across so
many disheartened Christians. Their cry is, "Surely there's more
than this?" They are not all rebellious, they want to live their life
in Christ to the full. Is this not what Jesus promised us?

Andrea and I are committed to seeing a change in this
mentality, particularly in the French speaking nations. Our
School of Ministries (EDMF) is a response to the desire to see
France and the other French speaking nations enter into all the
fullness of what God has for them. In order to achieve this, we
are convinced that more Christians need to leave the shadow
and enter into the substance of what they are called to be. Here
in England many have received the revelation that they needed
and have started their walk towards the substance.

I would like to end this book with a quote. Others who have gone before us have seen the shadow of a bigger picture for France. General De Gaulle was one of them. Whilst based in London, on June 18, 1940, he said the following:

"The leaders, who, for many years past, have been at the head of the French Armed forces, have set up a government. Alleging the defeat of our armies, this government has entered into negotiations with the enemy with a view to bringing about a cessation of hostilities. It is quite true that we were, and still are, overwhelmed by enemy mechanised forces, both on the ground and in the air. It was the tanks, the planes, and the tactics of the Germans, far more than the fact that we were outnumbered, that forced our armies to retreat. It was the German tanks, planes, and tactics that provided the element of surprise which brought our leaders to their present plight. But has the last word been said? Must we abandon all hope? Is our defeat final and irremediable? To those questions I answer No! Speaking in full knowledge of the facts, I ask you to believe me when I say that the cause of France is not lost. The very factors that brought about our defeat may one day lead us to victory. For France does not stand alone, remember this. She is not isolated. Behind her is a vast Empire, and she can make common cause with the British Empire, which commands the seas and is continuing the struggle. Like England, she can draw unreservedly on the immense industrial resources of the United States.

This war is not limited to our unfortunate country. The outcome of the struggle has not been decided by the Battle of France. This is a world war. Mistakes have been made, there have been delays and untold suffering, but the fact remains that there still exists in the world everything we need to crush our enemies some day. Today we are crushed by the sheer weight of mechanised force hurled against us, but we can still look to a future in which even greater mechanised forces will bring us victory. The destiny of the world is at stake.

I, General de Gaulle, now in London, call on all French officers and men, who are at present on British soil, or may be in the future, with or without their arms; I call on all engineers and skilled workmen from the armaments factories who are at present on British soil, or may be in the future, to get in touch with me.

Whatever happens, the flame of French resistance must not and shall not die.

Tomorrow I shall broadcast again from London.

General De Gaulle

He had seen the natural, we have seen the spiritual. He had seen the shadow, we have seen the substance. Together let us move towards it.

Acknowledgments

This portion normally comes at the beginning of a book, but with the publisher's permission and given the theme of the book, I want to end by drawing a distinction between those who have helped me in the shadow stage of my life and those who helped me and are still doing so as I try to live in the substance of what the Lord has called me to do.

► *I want to thank those who helped me in the shadow:*
My Dad for inspiring me and teaching me how to speak the language of drums and percussion. Dad you saw something of yourself in me and you knew how to feed my insatiable appetite for music. You have taught me the discipline of long hours of practice.

My sisters for putting up with an invasive and very loud brother!

Mr Roman and Miss Ferrier, my school music teachers. You saw my potential and helped me to develop it. Without Miss Ferrier, I would not be where I am today. Thank you for your persistence, for putting up with me, and accepting to go the extra mile for me.

All my PE teachers who showed me the healthy side of competition through sport.

Michel Visse (Percussion teacher CNR, Grenoble), Francis Brana (Percussion teacher CNR, Creteil) and Jacques Delecluse (Percussion teacher CNSM, Paris) for sharpening my iron and for opening my mind and ears to new sounds and textures.

Billy Hart and Keith Copeland for pushing me to the limit and broadening my horizon.

Olivier Messiaen for taking us to the pinnacle of musical expression.

My students, Christophe Torion, Alexandre Berrard and all the rest of them for making my time as a percussion teacher a delight and a learning curve.

Finally to all my friends, Jean Pierre Comparato, Benoit Sourisse, Bob Revel, Pierre Drevet, Philippe Roche, Jean Cohen ... to name but a few, and others in Grenoble, Lyon and Chambery for all the great moments with you on stage.

It is impossible to name everybody. Forgive me if you are not on this list but should be!

▶ *I also want to thank those who have helped me and those who still help me to live in the substance of God's calling:*
Jean Pierre Comparato for all your prayers. Louisa De Abdullah for leading me to Jesus. Robert Radix for your patience through my first steps as a young believer.

Chris Bowater for believing in me and for stretching my concept of worship. Trevor Jones, my father-in-law, for your example of integrity and for your wisdom. David Shearman for your inspiration and your prophetic insights into my life. Sylvain Freymond for your loyalty and your great example of integrity. Andrew Belfield for your support. Malcolm Baxter for the great times together. Tim Pettingale, my publisher, for believing in me, for your friendship. I always remember our deep conversations. Pastor Eric Maddison for giving me an appetite for the deep things of God. Liliane Payet, Marie Laure Fenet and Joelle Lepelletier for helping me to put this work together. Our friends in Israel, Karen, David, Peter, Brandon and many others for your love and support.

I want to thank you Andrea, my wife, for believing in me and for your constant support and love. Above all, I want to thank Jesus my Lord and my mediator for coming into my life, for inspiring the theme of this book and for taking me from the shadow to the substance.

About the Author

Gabriel was born in Annecy, France. His father was a drummer and first inspired Gabriel to pick up a pair of drum sticks. His love for drumming grew and at the age of eleven he began studying at the local conservatoire. It was there that he was introduced to classical percussion and orchestral work. His passion for music and percussion grew and he was awarded the gold medal in percussion from Grenoble conservatoire.

From there he progressed to the conservatoire in Creteil, Paris where he also was awarded the gold medal and was offered a place in the Conservatoire National Superieur de Musique in Paris under the tutelage of Jacques Delecluse. He graduated with first class honours along with his certificate for teaching.

He was subsequently appointed head of percussion in the conservatoire in Grenoble, drum and percussion teacher in the Jazz school in Chambery and was timpanist for the Orchestra of Grenoble. He held these posts until 1993. His musical career had so far taken him all over the world studying , teaching and performing jazz, classical and contemporary styles.

It was during a trip to South America that Gabriel was

touched by the Gospel. The revelation of Christ completely transformed his life and he left France in 1993, moving to England where he studied at a Bible school. Following this he joined the leadership team of the "Leadership Training School" in Nottingham and also began to travel to different nations sharing the Word of God.

Gabriel is now based in the North of England with his wife Andrea and they serve a local church (Five Towns Christian Fellowship). He is director and founder of EdMF (Ecole des Ministeres Francophones) a school of ministry for French-speaking leaders, based in England. He and Andrea travel to many nations serving the body of Christ through music and preaching. Gabriel is also a music arranger and producer and continues to play at a professional level.

We hope you enjoyed reading this New Wine book.
For details of other New Wine books
and a range of 2,000 titles from other
Spirit-filled publishers visit our website:
www.newwineministries.co.uk